This vault is on the left of that which runs down in a funnel shape from Smithdown Lane. The hole seen on the right leads to a labyrinth of vaults and strange passages.

©1998 Jim Moore

Published by
The Bluecoat Press
Liverpool

ISBN 1 872568 43 2

Book Design by
March Design
Liverpool

Acknowledgements

It is remarkable how many people have been prepared to give so much time and assistance
for this undertaking. Some of the individuals listed below have given up hours to explain the
topics outlined in this book in an attempt to instruct me in their specialist area. They have
also devoted hours checking the work which was full of inaccuracies and mistakes. There
are still no doubt many errors and I must take responsibility for those errors which no doubt
appear despite their checking.

I would like to thank:
Dr Nicky Ion for the use of the bibliography from her PhD thesis on "The Causes and Effects
of Rising Groundwater in Merseyside and Manchester". Neville King who formerly worked
for North West Water and Peter Cahill of North West Water spent hours assisting and
checking my work. Joe Spiers, Andy Kidd and Martin Hutchinson of Liverpool City Engineers
provided invaluable assistance on sewers. The staff at Sandon Dock Sewage Works. Steve
Kelly and Paul Crane at the Environment Agency for information on boreholes and well
licences. Richard Duncombe and Trevor Harden from Halcrow Engineering Consultants for
information on the new wells being sunk to drain the Mersey Rail Loop Line. Nick Porter and
Joe Kehoe of British Rail and Merseyrail Electrics Ltd for information on underground
railways. Peter Arch for information on the Mersey Tunnels. John Howells of Liverpool
University and Rob Cuss a graduate of the Geology Department of Liverpool University. Rob
Cuss carried out a gravity survey of the Williamson tunnels. Bernard Jones of Parkman
Associates for maps of surveys of the Williamson tunnels. Gabriel Muies and The Friends of
Joseph Williamson who are equally passionate about Joseph Williamson and the need to
preserve his tunnels. Combined Operations Headquarters for use of their map. Anastasia
Mc Crave and the staff at the Postal Sorting Office at Copperas Hill. Margaret Davies and
Peter Madren at MANWEB for information on Liverpool's Electricity Supply. Sandra Black at
British Gas and D Swannick at Transco Gas for information on gas supplies. Walter Bunn for
information on the underground stores under Exchange Flags. Dave Hurst at Potters Book
Shop. Bob McClennan at Liverpool Metropolitan Cathedral. David Felgate of Liverpool
Anglican Cathedral. Judy Gilpin, a student at St Julie's Roman Catholic High School. Philip
Browning, for his work on St George's Hall, and to the staff of St George's Hall who
showed me around the nether regions of this fine building.

Special thanks must go to Stan Roberts who provided enormous quantities of information
and who checked much the text. Lisa Jackson helped with much of the early material and
her research has made a great contribution to this book. Angela Mounsey and Liz
Wilkinson for their patience in editing the text and Michael March for the design. Special
thanks should also go to the staff at Liverpool Record Office and the Karen Howard of
NMGM Special Collections for providing information and photographs.

Apologies go to all those people whose contribution has not been acknowledged here. My
records were not kept quite as assiduously as they should have been and so many people
provided assistance that I am sure that someone has been omitted.

Printed by
Ashford Colour Press,
Gosport, Hants

Underground Liverpool

Jim Moore

The Bluecoat Press

The shape of Liverpool

Liverpool's urban landscape – some 111 square kilometres of buildings and roads – masks its natural hills and valleys, streams and marshlands and its shoreline of sand and low cliffs. It has taken just a few hundred years for this natural landscape to disappear, but we can get some idea of Liverpool's former self and its development from old illustrations of the city.

In 1625, Liverpool was confined to a low ridge on which stood the Castle. However, the growth of the shipping trade made Liverpool one of the fastest growing cities in the world. The demand for land and housing was insatiable and areas of land were incorporated into Liverpool at various times during the nineteenth and twentieth centuries. Villages such as Walton and Wavertree were swallowed up and their rural aspects changed. The last major expansion took place in Speke in 1952 but, even after this, Liverpool continued to grow by invading neighbouring districts with housing estates.

The highest point in Liverpool today is Woolton Hill which, with its woodland cover, resembles the landscape of hundreds of years ago. Woolton is only one of a number of ridges which run from north to south. The ancient castle was easily defended by the prominence of the most westerly of these ridges, Sand Hill and Bevington Hill, which ran south along the coast from Bootle boundary to the Pool.

Between the coastal ridge and the much steeper Everton Hill, is a valley which is a continuation of the Pool. In fact, Everton Ridge runs all the way down to Toxteth, where it ends in a steep slope overlooking the river. These steep slopes presented early obstacles to development as trams and trains found the west facing scarp hard to negotiate.

Deep cuttings, tunnels and embankments were needed to maintain a low gradient for the railways. Routes were chosen which sought to avoid the steepest gradients. The arrival of trains in the centre of Liverpool was delayed by the need to build costly tunnels from Edge Hill and Crown Street to Lime Street. These tunnels helped to reduce the gradients but winches were still needed in the early days.

The few maps which still exist show that short, steep streams, some with familiar names such as Kirkdale Brook and Bootle Brook, ran down the coastal scarp slope straight into the Mersey. They were important sources of water, especially the springs at the Fall Well and Bootle Well. Names like Dingle and Otterspool go back to the days when small streams were a common feature. The inland plateau drained south into Ditton Brook which reaches the Mersey near Widnes. Tewbrook, a name still familiar to all Liverpudlians, joins the Alt at Fazakerley and flows north to enter Liverpool Bay near Formby.

Not only did the old shoreline change, but it extended over 100 metres into the river in many places. The Dock Road behind the Liver Building is called the Strand for obvious reasons and the Pierhead, like most of the dockland, is 'made' ground. The largest of the inlets was the Pool which has also disappeared to be replaced by Whitechapel, Paradise Street and Canning Place.

Many people regret these changes and the apparent disappearance of the landscape. In fact, it has not gone and the hills and streams are still there. They cannot be seen very easily, but anyone who cycles up Childwall Valley Road or Everton Brow will be left in no doubt. The streams both above and below ground need careful management in case they flood or suffer pollution. Attempts to recreate or retain the past with new parks and village preservation schemes are commendable but many changes are permanent and part of the changing face of Liverpool.

Opposite In Everton, the main roads tend to run from north to south along the valley (Netherton Road) and the ridge (Heyworth Street) avoiding the scarp. Everton Brow runs straight down the steep scarp. A plateau spreads out far to the east. It rises gently to a ridge at Olive Mount and Childwall which runs straight down to Woolton. The eastern side of this ridge is also very steep and the main roads which descend to Childwall Valley made urban expansion in this area difficult, especially for the tram. Road transport had no such difficulty. Despite this many main roads tend to run from north to south (Barnham Drive and Grange Lane).

Below A view of Everton Brow. The skyline is dominated by hedged fields and windmills taking advantage of the open heights facing the sea. This landscape has been partly restored with the creation of a new park in Everton.

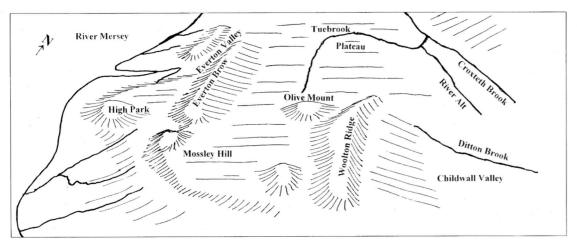

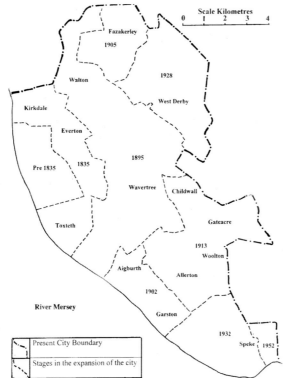

Above To the north, Everton Hill fell away to a broad undulating plateau across which flowed Liverpool's larger streams. This diagram shows them as they may have been two thousand years ago.

Right A map showing the expansion of Liverpool.

Far right Children at play on the steep streets of Everton.

Scale Kilometres
0 1 2 3 4

	Present City Boundary
	Stages in the expansion of the city

The building blocks of Liverpool

The Triassic Sandstones

In an age when we have put men on the moon and we have space ships travelling to the furthest corners of the solar system and beyond, our knowledge of what lies beneath our feet is remarkably scant.

Most people know that Liverpool is built on sandstone. This sandstone was formed during the Triassic period about 200 million years ago when Britain probably lay somewhere on the tropics and was covered by a desert not unlike the Sahara.

If you visit the Sahara today, you will find barren, rocky hills with ephemeral streams which pour their infrequent torrents over a lowland plain and empty into salt lakes. Sand dunes migrate over these plains and, as there is little water, life is sparse.

This is a good description of the conditions in which the sandstones of Merseyside formed. Powerful rivers carrying hard, quartzite pebbles flowed north from the barren hills of the Midlands. These pebbles are found scattered throughout certain layers in the sandstone but are less abundant in Merseyside than further south in Cheshire. It took a lot of rubbing to round off these hard pebbles which are frequently used for rough paving and cobbles. Current bedding in the sandstones shows that the river currents tended to flow in many different directions as the river channels meandered over the plain. Good examples can be seen in many rock outcrops such as those in Woolton, Everton Hill and Thurstaston Common. Look at any sandstone wall in Liverpool and you are almost certain to see contortions that were made by slump structures. If sand comes to rest at even slight angles on the edge of a sand bank in a river, it frequently slips down the face of the sand bank and the layers roll up into slump structures. The best examples of slump structures in Merseyside are probably those located in the road cutting of the A 540 below Thurstaston Hill. The sand dunes in this area were tens of metres high and are best represented in the railway cutting at Frodsham. The dune layers slope to the west, indicating that the wind blew from the east at that time. Deserts today are characterised by consistent trade winds from the east. Dune bedding is not so well represented in Liverpool itself but whilst we may have an image of vast sand dunes in the desert they are not necessarily typical, even in the Sahara, where they only make up a fraction of the desert landscape. Lakes filled with salt were extensive in Cheshire and the Cheshire Salt Mines supply the country with salt. These lakes must have been very persistent as the layers of salt under Cheshire are many metres thick around the town of Northwich. Boreholes in Liverpool do not penetrate salt layers but fragments of the mineral gypsum and salt pseudomorphs are not uncommon. We have indications of the arid nature of the past landscape in the desiccation cracks which can be found in the sandstone. We occasionally find such cracks in muddy surfaces which dry and shrink in a hot summer. Dessication cracks formed where the sand of a river or lake bed dried out and shrank in the same way. Dust filled the cracks and was squeezed up into ridges as the sand became moist once more.

From looking at the many quarries, road cuttings, tunnels and boreholes, we can reconstruct the former Triassic desert environment. Even deserts have life and this desert was not totally barren. The plants that once grew have left their leaf remains on some of the Merseyside rock layers, in particular the Keuper Waterstones. The only animals we know of in this part of Cheshire were dinosaurs which wandered across the flood plains of the rivers and the lake beds. Their footprints have been found in large numbers in Storeton Quarry and sets of prints can be seen in the Liverpool Museum, the Wirral Country Park Visitors Centre at Thurstaston and the Department of Geology at the University of Liverpool. These dinosaurs were quite modest in size.

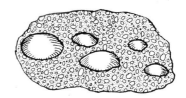

Bunter pebbles, derived from the German word 'bunt' meaning colourful.

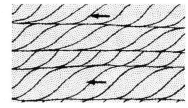

Current bedding, showing the directional flow of meandering river channels.

Slump bedding. the layering and slumping of sand on sandbanks.

Dune bedding, showing the direction of the wind at the tim the layers were deposited.

Salt pseudomorphs, fragments of which can be found along with the mineral gypsum.

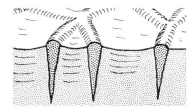

Mud cracks: dessication cracks that are found in Liverpool's sandstone give an indication of the arid nature of the past landscape.

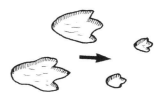

Chirotherium footprints, a dinosaur about the size of a cow which wandered across the floodplains of river and lake beds.

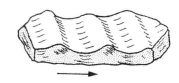

Ripple marks.

Liverpool during the coal foaming conditions of the Upper Carboniferous period.

Liverpool during the desert conditions of the Triassic period.

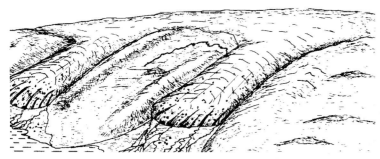

Liverpool during the Ice Age.

Chirotherium was about the size of a cow and Rhyncosaurus, the size of a dog. We can only speculate about their appearance as they have left no solid remains, unlike those found in abundance in the famous dinosaur graveyards of the United States. Both dinosaurs and mammals were in their infancy at this time and were not very common.

During the nineteenth century, the geologists gave these rocks names to match their vibrant colours. The official geological names have changed but a frequent visitor to the museum will be more familiar with the old, more colourful names. The Bunter series, derived from the German word 'bunt', meaning 'colourful', includes the Pebble Beds and a series of sandstones called the Mottled Sandstones. The Bunter series is generally made up of hard rocks and makes up much of the high ground in Liverpool such as the hills of Woolton and Everton. The Keuper series is derived from the German word 'kupfer' meaning copper, which is found in shales of this age in Germany. Very little of the Keuper is found in Liverpool. There are, however, a large number of north-south normal faults within the city limits. They are probably Tertiary in age. The main faults lie near the eastern boundary of the city and near the Mersey shore. They may well have helped to form the steep slopes of Woolton Hill and Everton Brow. The faults caused severe problems for the contractors working on the Mersey tunnels.

The sandstones are both porous and permeable and therefore have played an important part in Liverpool's water supply. Because of this, many boreholes have been sunk and records from these have provided us with a reasonable idea of what lies beneath our feet.

The deep boreholes

One of the deepest of these boreholes was sunk near Croxteth Park in 1952 by Steel Brothers Ltd who were searching for oil and gas. This borehole was sunk half a mile west of Croxteth Hall to a depth of 4,216ft 6ins and cut the Croxteth Fault itself. The first 357ft penetrated 125ft of recent sands and clays and 232ft of glacial sands and clays. Given that the height of the site above sea-level was 84ft, this gives a below sea-level depth for the glacial iceway of 273ft, which almost matches the Dee hollow. Another 1,306ft penetrated Triassic sandstone. Most of this was probably Bunter sands and there were thin marls and gypsum between 700 and 900ft. Lack of fossils makes precise dating of the rocks difficult. The rest of the borehole is in Carboniferous rocks. The coal measures were missed, as they lie to the east in the 'inlier' nearer the surface. There were nearly 2,000ft of Millstone Grit, a series of sands and shales which are found extensively in the Pennines. The final 616ft were in Carboniferous limestone which was found to be rich in fossil fragments with veins of zinc and lead. The dip of the rocks was about 25° and the beds had been fractured and deformed by the nearby Croxteth fault. The rocks and fossils in the borehole suggest a Carboniferous environment of shallow seas in which limestone accumulated in a manner similar to that in which the reefs of the Pennines and Wales formed. This came as something of a surprise as, in the deep Formby Borehole, sediments were found which were formed in a much deeper marine environment. There is no record of oil and gas being found but drilling offshore in Liverpool Bay has been much more successful.

The Carboniferous rocks

The Croxteth Park Inlier is one of two brought up to the surface by the Croxteth Park Fault. This fault has brought up middle coal measures which have been mined extensively in the better-exposed Lancashire Coalfield to the east. The coal measures include sandstones, shales and coal seams. The conditions under which these rocks were formed were very different from those of the Triassic sandstone. In Lancashire at this time, dense forests grew in tropical swamps. River channels cut though these swamps such as might be found today in areas like the Niger and Ganges deltas. Periodically, the forests would be destroyed by floods which buried them under layers of sand. At other times, the swampy areas subsided, allowing the sea to flood in and drown the forests. Layers of mud, rich in marine fossils, were deposited and these sediments would bury the trees and the pressure converted them into coal.

The rocks shape the landscape and economy

The sands and clays have proved economically very useful and have been quarried extensively in Lancashire and Liverpool. Stone-built houses in Lancashire tend to be an orange brown, the colour of the Carboniferous sandstones, in contrast to the bright Triassic sandstones of Liverpool. Both types of stone tend to become blackened by smoke and soot from the age of coal-fuelled transport but as the grime spalls off and buildings are cleaned, the contrast becomes obvious. Many of the older houses in the city centre and the outlying villages are made of this red Triassic sandstone. Woolton once had a thriving quarrying industry which employed thousands but the high cost of stone and widespread use of brick, forced its closure, although the construction of the Anglican Cathedral kept the industry and skills going until recently. Some of the quarries have been infilled but others remain. The one in Quarry Street, Woolton, has even provided the site for a new housing development.

The Ice Age

The most extensive deposit lying on the surface of Liverpool is Boulder Clay or Till. This is a glacial deposit dumped as the glaciers melted and retreated and is found mainly in the valleys but also on the plateaux. As the name implies, it consists of a mixture of rocks and clay. For gardeners, digging this clay can be hard going. The rocks in the clay

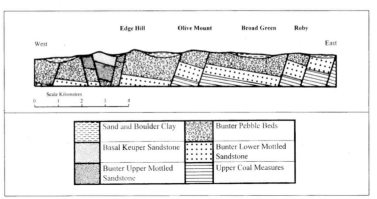

left *Morton's cross-section shows the rocks of Liverpool are broken up by numerous faults and capped by patches of glacial deposits.*

can frequently be recognised as far-travelled 'erratics' such as Granite and Volcanic rocks, brought down by the ice sheets from the Lake District. The boulders are often angular and carry scratches showing how they chafed against each other. Thurstaston Beach is a particularly good place to find them and there is a very good example of an andesitic agglomerate in front of Picton Road Library. Local children tend to call it a meteorite but it is actually made up of fragments of volcanic ash from the Borrowdale Volcanic series in the Lake District, dug up at Gypsy Lane in Childwall. Higher areas have few recent surface deposits as the ice followed the lower ground and exposures of solid rock are more common in higher areas.

Recent deposits

The coastal areas have a belt of sands appropriately located at locations like Sandhills. Similar sands further inland are older and blew inland thousands of years ago. A local name for these sands is the Shirdley Hill Sands, so important for the glass industry in St Helens. They also provide light fertile soils which are much easier to dig.

Melting glaciers produce large quantities of sand and gravel which are easily recognised from blown sands because of the larger pebbles mixed in with them. The gravels differ from the boulder clay because the pebbles are more rounded than the glacial boulders. There are very few gravels within the Liverpool boundary but in Lancashire and Wales they are a vital source of aggregates.

Alluvium is a mud deposited by rivers which can be found along the Mersey shore and in the valleys of the larger streams such as the Alt and Ditton.

Where have all the rivers gone?

The answer is they are still there. The map below shows the pattern of rivers as found on old maps of the Liverpool area but accurate, large-scale maps of areas outside the centre of Liverpool are rare. The first useful map was probably produced by Yates and Perry in 1768 but the scale of half inch to one mile is too small to give adequate detail and its accuracy is limited. Sherriff produced a map of Liverpool in 1816 which covered an area which extended as far as St Helens, Widnes and Ormskirk. As already pointed out, Liverpool at this time was confined to a small nucleus located between Edge Hill and the old Pool. All the main rivers are depicted on Sherriff's map and most streams are named after a local area. Even Kirkdale and Bootle Brooks were located in the countryside at this time.

The watersheds run along the crests of the ridges and the streams which ran into the river Mersey were little more than small brooks. The rivers at the south end of Liverpool such as the Jordan River with its tributaries, the Upper and Lower Brooks, drained a much larger catchment area. Two larger, unnamed streams ran into the Mersey Estuary at Garston and, like other streams in the Liverpool area, one of the Garston streams had a water mill, complete with water wheel and millpond. The plateau was drained by Tew Brook now spelt Tuebrook. The large glacial iceway to the east of Liverpool had the largest streams in the area and these included the River Alt, Croxteth Brook and Ditton and Childwall Brooks. Today, Croxteth Brook and several of the Ditton tributaries form the boundary of the City of Liverpool.

Opposite Sadly many of our rivers now flow in culverts. Here the River Alt is being boxed in concrete.

Far left The pattern of rivers as found on old maps of the Liverpool area but accurate, large-scale maps of areas outside the centre of Liverpool are rare

Left This map shows the streams as they are today although accurate information is hard to obtain.

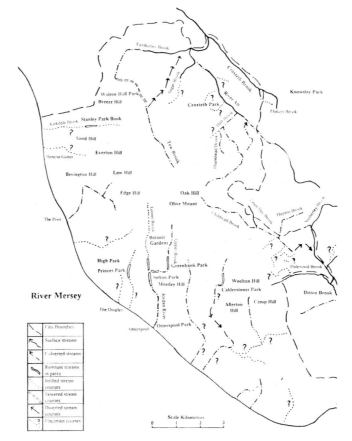

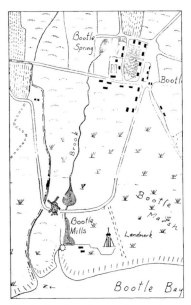

The Bootle wells and springs dominated Liverpool's water supply. For many years people would visit Bootle 'the bath of Merseyside'.

Some of the brooks in Liverpool were fed by springs, the most important of which were Bootle Springs and the Fall Well. As boreholes and wells were sunk into the sandstone and water was drawn off in increasing quantities, the water table gradually fell and the springs, and probably some of the smaller streams, stopped flowing.

The larger streams such as Ditton Brook, the River Alt and Croxteth Brook continue to flow on the surface. Croxteth Brook and the River Alt, where it flows through Croxteth Country Park, are probably the most natural streams in appearance. The River Alt starts as an open brook in Huyton and flows under Liverpool Road. The open section along the Huyton Link Road is grassy but hardly natural having been straightened. At the time of writing, it is being relandscaped in an attempt to recapture its former appearance. Culverted under parts of West Derby, it reappears beside the appropriately named 'Brookside' and then flows through Croxteth Park. It remains on the surface until it reaches the East Lancashire Road, where it is once more culverted, reappearing beside Fazakerley sewage works. Where it does flow on the surface, there are seldom houses located in the immediate vicinity, as the Alt has been known to flood. The Alt had a few small tributaries in 1816 although most are omitted on Sherriff's map. Deys Brook is one of the largest tributaries and part of it still flows on the surface, mainly through West Derby golf course. The rest of the stream, together with Hall Brook and Thurnhead Brook, is culverted. The south side of Fazakerley sewage works is bordered by Sugar Brook, the lower section of which is still on the surface.

The main tributary of the Alt is Tuebrook which starts near Prescot Road and is culverted all the way to Fazakerley with the exception of a short surface section behind the North West Water depot on Green Lane. Unlike other streams it is then diverted along a tunnel to cut off the large Fazakerley loop and is then 'sewered'. This can only be done where water flows are small unless the sewers are specifically built to take flood discharge. Water continues to flow into the Tew Brook water course and by the time it gets to Walton, a surface stream is once again in existence, flowing east, just south of Fazakerley hospital with a much-reduced flow. Part of Tew Brook flows under what was once open ground between Richard Kelly Drive and Abingdon Road. It is common practice not to build on culverted streams but, nevertheless, houses and a new Asda have been built on this open space.

Most of the small, short streams flowing down to the river have no surface course or culvert, the exception being the old Pool stream which is now culverted. Kirkdale Brook and Beacon Gutter may well have dried up as the water table fell, although Stanley Park lake lies along the course of the old Kirkdale Brook. The practice of laying out parks incorporating natural features such as hills, valleys and streams is an old and logical one. Nowhere is this more apparent than in the Jordan River and the Upper and Lower Brooks. The brooks both start near Smithdown Road and the Upper Brook is culverted until it reaches Greenbank Park where it has been dammed to form Greenbank Lake. It then continues under Greenbank Lane into the Greenbank university halls of residence complex where there is another lake. A culvert takes it into Sefton Park where the wrought iron bridge takes Mossley Hill Drive over a stream section which has been landscaped into a series of gardens and pools. Several years ago, a popular Sunday outing for families was to go and feed the rats on the islands in the stream. The main lake in Sefton Park was built at the confluence of the two brooks and the smaller northern lakes lie in the Lower Book course. Princes Park lake also lies on an old water course.

Aigburth Vale derives its name from the stream course which now runs through a culvert under the road. The older culverts are brick-arched tunnels and, over the course of time, these arches tend to collapse (square concrete culverts and large concrete pipes tend to last longer). The section of culvert under Jericho Lane consists of smaller double arches to take the weight of traffic which is probably responsible for the collapse of other culverts in Liverpool. Having crossed Aigburth Road, the water course flows into Otterspool Park as an open stream and then goes underground once more where a number of surface drains add to the discharge into the Mersey Estuary at Otterspool Promenade.

One of the unnamed streams which flows into Garston includes Calderstones Park and lake along its length. The greater part of the northern branch of this stream is culverted. The middle section, however, does not match the old surface water course, as it has been diverted towards the Mersey and now flows along the Allerton railway line. The southern branch of this stream has a culvert section at its source in Woolton but it is hard to trace its full course.

Ditton Brook still flows on the surface for much of its length but its source near Childwall Church is interesting. Sherriff's map shows a source at Oak Hill near Broadgreen with a stream flowing south to join Court Hey Brook. It then flows underground along a culvert until it reaches Court Hey Park. Court Hey Brook flows on the surface through the park and at the footbridge from Childwall Valley Road through to Bowring Park, it enters a culvert which has a large grill covering its entrance. When heavy rain causes the level of flow to rise rapidly, twigs and plant debris quickly block the culvert grill and floods are not uncommon. Much of this debris appears to come from householders who throw garden rubbish into the stream. Numerous complaints about pollution and smells have been made and consequent studies have put the cause down to householders who install washing machines and run foul water into storm water drains which in turn run into the brook. The culvert runs along the Liverpool boundary behind the houses in Belle Vale. Like Richard Kelly Drive, this area until recently remained without houses. Now houses and a new road have been built on top of the culvert.

Sherriff's map also shows a 'bath' below the church. Could this be a spring which has now dried up? Until recently, a pond locally called Jackson's Pond lay between the former railway line in Childwall Valley and Barnham Drive. This was almost certainly spring fed and was popular with local youths for fishing. A park now stands on the site of the pond and the ground remains wet. Water constantly seeps from the fields at Barnham Drive into Childwall Valley Road where the railway bridge crosses the road. Has the railway impeded the natural drainage? The culvert taking Childwall Brook is joined by several tributaries. Huyton Brook is culverted but the smaller streams shown on Sherriff's map cannot be traced. Near the sewage works in Halewood, Childwall Brook has been diverted from its original course. It soon emerges from its underground course and is joined by the surface streams of Netherley Brook and Halewood Brook as its leaves Liverpool.

There is little chance of restoring the streams to their former rural tranquillity, but they can be kept clean. The sewage works at Fazakerley and Halewood discharge treated water into the River Alt and Ditton Brook respectively with relatively little harm, but what of the streams which cannot be traced? Some may have been routed along sewers while others have just been buried. They clearly have not caused major problems in the past but as the water table rises, will they begin to flow again? Should people who now live over a water course be concerned?

The Jordan River still survives despite extensive culverting and provides the central feature for several parks, including Sefton Park, seen here in its Victorian heyday.

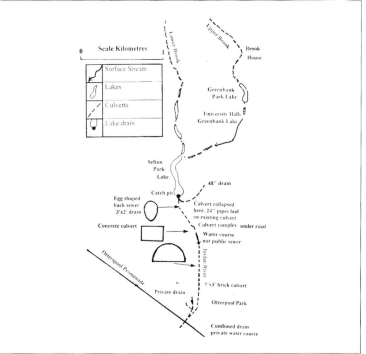

Underground lakes and wells

When people speak of underground lakes they may well imagine a large body of water such as can be found in underground limestone caverns in Derbyshire or the Mendip Hills. The term can be used for the water in the ground under Liverpool but it does not take the form of a lake. What people mean is that the rock is porous and contains large quantities of water. The sandstones of Liverpool have a porosity of around 30%. This has little meaning unless the rock is permeable, i.e. water will move through the rock. The local sandstones are both porous and permeable and provided Liverpool with the bulk of its water up until the early 1800s. Numerous fissures run through the sandstone and allow the water to move rapidly in some places.

This groundwater has an upper surface called the 'water table'. The shape of the water table resembles the land surface. If the land is steep, the water table is also steep which gives it a head. Where the water table breaks the land surface, springs occur which used to feed the streams flowing down to the Mersey shore. The Fall Well was the most famous of these springs and was located near St George's Hall. It is reckoned that the whole town was supplied with about 100,000 gallons of water per day. The water was distributed by hand or cart and a small reservoir was located at the well for washing etc. As the town grew, the water supplies from the Fall Well proved inadequate and extra water had to be brought in from the Bootle wells located to the north of the town. Some accounts record that there were 2,000 springs in Bootle.

In 1786, an Act of Parliament was passed to provide extra water from new wells and wells were sunk in Berry Street, Hotham Street and Copperas Hill. Pipes distributed the water and the water carts became unnecessary. Intense competition existed between the Bootle Water Company and the Liverpool and Harrington Water Company. At the Bootle Water Works, three large lodges were excavated to a depth of 23ft and eleven boreholes were sunk to depths varying from 63 to 600ft. Steam engines raised and distributed the water. The Liverpool and Harrington Water Company had five sets of wells at Bevington Bush, Copperas Hill, Soho, Toxteth Park and Windsor Street, the depths of which reached 256ft.

In the 1840s, the water supply from these wells was proving inadequate and the water mains were too small. A new deep well was sunk at Green Lane in Old Swan and the water was piped to Kensington Reservoir. Most wells have now been abandoned as salt water has intruded from the Mersey and the quality of the ground water

Opposite Old wells are occasionally discovered during building work. Here a well in Everton is uncovered during the 1930s.

Left Recording a well discovered in the city centre in the 1960s

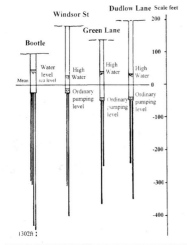

Above The cross at Monks Well marks the site of a spring which fed a lake in the middle of Wavertree. Both the well and the lake have roads named after them.

Top The deepest holes on Liverpool are the large 19th century wells

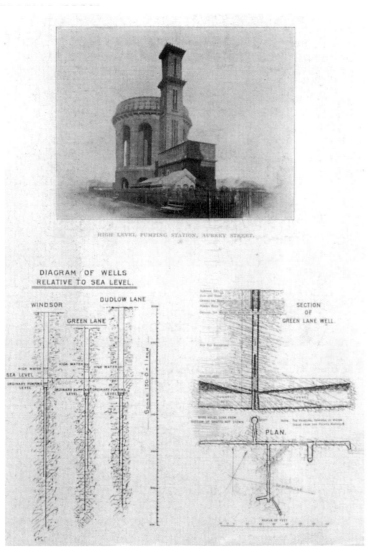

HIGH LEVEL PUMPING STATION, AUBREY STREET.

DIAGRAM OF WELLS
RELATIVE TO SEA LEVEL.

SECTION OF GREEN LANE WELL.

PLAN.

Green Lane Well is quite complicated with four shafts reaching 185ft. As in other major wells, headings were driven out from the base to extend the supply area. Two boreholes continue down from the base of the main well; the first is a 7ins shaft to 199ft and the second is an 18ins bore to 310ft giving a total depth of 520ft.

has deteriorated. Rapid urban growth meant continued pressure on available water supplies and two new large wells were opened at Bootle (1869) and Dudlow Lane (1870). The new Bootle Well was sunk to a depth of 1302ft and had a diameter of 24ins but it did not yield as much water as anticipated despite galleries cut laterally into the sandstone which tapped numerous fissures. The use of the Bootle wells ceased when the Vyrnwy water supplies came on stream. The well is still there together with roads named Waterworks Street, Mill Lane, Brookhill Road, Brook Close and Well Lane.

The Windsor Street Well was sunk to 210ft with an oval cross section 12ft by 10ft. Headings were driven out from the base of this well in order to increase the flow of water. Two 6ins boreholes were sunk to depths of 244 and 380ft respectively. The hot water from the steam pump which raised the water was used for Lodge Lane baths.

Green Lane Well is even more complicated with four shafts reaching 185ft. As in other major wells, headings were driven out from the base to extend the supply area. Two boreholes continue down from the base of the main well. The first borehole is a 7ins shaft to 199ft and second an 18ins bore to 310ft giving a total depth of 520ft.

Dudlow Lane Well had two oval shafts 12ft by 9ft to a depth of 247ft. Again headings were driven out sideways from the base of this well and two boreholes were sunk. One was 18ins in diameter and went down to a depth of 196ft and the other had a 6in diameter and a depth of 300ft giving a total depth of 547ft.

As time went on, the yield of water from the wells declined and the quality of the water deteriorated with an increase in water hardness. Even by 1918, the wells had greater quantities of solutes such as nitrates and chlorides than when they were first dug. Sewering and paving alleviated the contamination a little but heavy pumping from the Mersey tunnels has tended to deplete fresh water levels near the Mersey estuary. Indeed, the wells nearest the Mersey not only show higher salt water contamination levels but the water levels in some wells can be seen to rise and fall with the tides. This intrusion was at one time confined to the area around the Pool but Wedd reported in 1923 that the intrusion extended a mile inland.

But what of the underground lakes. The main Bootle shaft begun in 1799 is 11ft 9ins by 9ft and the holding chamber is 108ft below the surface. Adits and deeper shafts lead off this main chamber. There are 12 shallow boreholes and three deep boreholes which extend down hundreds of feet below sea-level. In 1878 The Corporation sunk the well which reached 1302ft deep. Reports in the Bootle Times in the early 1990s report that a boat was lowered into these chambers. In 1959, the water level was reported to be 65ft down in the shaft. It was probably above these large holding chambers. Some accounts suggest that there is a natural lake and others that the well cuts one or more faults. The Bunter Sandstone is not likely to form natural caverns such as one might expect in limestone areas. The well is now part-filled with sand and it would be costly to prove the size and extent of the 'underground lakes'. Divers who went down many years ago had limited success. The sinking of the wells had probably extinguished the springs.

Springs also existed on the other side of the city. Childwall Brook was fed by a spring once located near the junction of Well Lane and Score Lane, 200yds from the Childwall Abbey public house. This was known as the 'Monks Bath' and is shown on Sherriff's map of 1826. The water flowed down to the 'Cistern Pit' known locally as Jackson's Pond. The water of the well occupied a basin 15ft across. The well and spring dried up in 1840 when the Green Lane Well was sunk and the water table was lowered and the well was filled in. Roadworks at the corner of Score Lane and Well Lane carried out in 1965 found a well 4-5ft in diameter. Childwall may derive its name from the Norse word 'vellir' or 'meeting place' but, in the reign of Richard II, it was spelt 'Chidewell'. This may refer directly to the well, a very important feature of the land in the Middle Ages.

The only visible spring today is in St James Gardens to the east of the Anglican Cathedral. This spring is in the gardens which were previously a graveyard and, before that, a quarry. It would not have been there before the quarry and there are few references to it in geological and hydrological literature. It is reported to have medicinal qualities. The dissolved minerals may have provided a cure when little else was available.

The history of Liverpool's water has not been a complete success story. Cholera and typhoid epidemics hit Liverpool in the mid-1800s, coinciding with a rapid increase in population and resulting from foul waste leaking into water supplies. The years 1847-58 saw a major sewer building operation under the supervision of James Newlands, the City Engineer and the first roads were tarmaced in 1851. Rivington Water was flowing by 1862 and the disease was defeated by a combination of improved engineering, housing and medical work. Credit must also be given to Dr Thomas Duncan, Liverpool's Medical

The only visible spring today is in St James Gardens to the east of the Anglican Cathedral.

Above A graph showing a reconstruction of the water table as constructed by Rushton, Kawecki and Brassington (1985).

Right A map of the region showing the distribution of boreholes and wells.

Opposite A table cataloguing water usage in the Merseyside area.

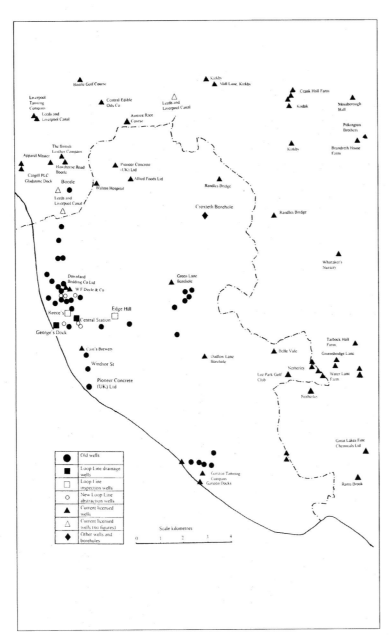

Officer of Health who was appointed following the passing of the Sanitary Act in 1847, the year James Newlands was appointed City Engineer. The causes of typhoid and cholera were not discovered until the 1880s but the improvements in water and sewers provided a cure before the cause was known. These diseases killed rich and poor but the rich could escape to the leafy country villages like Wavertree and Walton.

Well abstraction increased during the 19th Century. As a result, Liverpool's water table continued to fall and its quality deteriorated. The main consumer of water was industry and there are still wells and boreholes used by industry or available for use in emergencies. Well water is costly to abstract and the water table reached its lowest level in the 1960s. Since then pumping has declined. The water table is now rising again, a phenomenon common in other British cities such as Birmingham and London. At Edge Hill, the water table has been rising at 30cm per year. The rate of rise is now slowing as the water table is approaching its former levels. This is welcome news if your house stands on the site of an old spring or water course, as a significant rise could prove disastrous. Many tunnels now thread through the sandstone below Liverpool. The Mersey tunnels need to be kept dry and pumps were erected in both. The Loop Line has a special problem and leaks profusely. Weep holes allow the water to flow into the tunnel and the water drains down a channel in the floor of the tunnel to a sump and pump at Central station. The water is pumped out and sold to the Liverpool Daily Post and Echo and they sell hot water on to the Royal Insurance Company. Of the 1000 gallons per minute which flow into the Loop Line, 300 are pumped out at Central Station and the other 700 drain down to George's Dock and are pumped out there. This solves the water problem but corrosion is much higher in a wet tunnel than out in the open and repair costs on the Loop Line are extremely high, with lines needing to be replaced every two years instead of every 15-20 years. The inflow of water varies along the length of the Loop Line and is greatest at Lime Street where the line cuts a fault. The water is salty and particularly 'aggressive', causing corrosion of concrete and electricity leakage. The water can never be allowed to reach its former level as the tunnels would flood and existing boreholes, though they may not be used for abstraction, are still used to monitor ground water levels. This is particularly the case with the wells at Edge Hill and 'Reece's Restaurant'.

Company	Location	Annual Abstraction	Daily Abstraction	Use of water
North West Water	Netherley – 3 boreholes	4,127,000,000 litres	11,400,000 litres	Public Water Supply
North West Water	Belle Vale – 2 boreholes	1,573,000,000 litres	5,500,000 litres	Public Water Supply
North West Water	Greensbridge Lane – 2 boreholes	1,500,000,000 litres	11,400,000 litres	Public Water Supply
Water Lane Farm	Tarbock – 4 boreholes	1,700,000 gallons	100,000 gallons	Spray Irrigation
Tarbock Hall Farm	Tarbock – 2 boreholes	461,500 gallons	1,265 gallons	Spray Irrigation
North West Water	Rams Brook	3,000,000 gallons	24,000 gallons	Effluent Treatment
Dista Products	Fleming Road, Speke – 2 boreholes	157,000,000 gallons	480,000 gallons	Manufacturing
Garston Tanning Company	King Street, Garston	227,305,000 litres	1,000,000 litres	Manufacturing
Mossborough Hall	Farm, Rainford	4,200,000 gallons	16,000 gallons	Agriculture
Brandreth House Farm	Eccleston	1,000,000 gallons	30,000 gallons	Spray Irrigation
Whittaker's Nursery	Prescot	170,000 gallons	17,000 gallons	Other Irrigation
Pilkington Brothers	St Helens	350,000,000 gallons	1,152,000 gallons	Manufacturing
North West Water	Kirkby – 2 boreholes	1,659,326,000 litres	7,500,000 litres	Public Water Supply
North West Water	Kirkby	365,000,000 gallons	1,540,000 gallons	Public Water Supply
North West Water	Randles Bridge	455,000,000 gallons	1,980,000 gallons	Public Water Supply
Knowsley Metropolitan Borough	Mill Lane, Kirkby	100,000,000 gallons	530,000 gallons	Transfer of Water
Crank Hall Farm	Simonswood	10,000,000 gallons	220,000 gallons	Spray Irrigation
Kodak	Knowsley Industrial Estate	20,000,000 gallons	75,000 gallons	Industrial
Petrolite	Knowsley Industrial Park North	55,000,000 gallons	180,000 gallons	Industrial
Wincharn Investments	Hawthorne Road, Bootle	27,380,000 gallons	144,000 gallons	Manufacturing
The British Leather Company	Hawthorne Road, Bootle	35,000,000 gallons	150,000 gallons	Manufacturing
Liverpool Tanning Company	Field Lane, Litherland	136,363,000 litres	600,000 litres	Manufacturing
WF Doyle & Co	Haileybury Road, Blackstock Street	299,905,000 litres	2,182,000 litres	Cooling water
North West Water	Green Lane Borehole	1,050,000,000 gallons	3,100,000 gallons	Public Water Supply
	Dudlow Lane Borehole			
British Waterways Board	Leeds & Liverpool Canal – 5 boreholes	0	0	NA
Fairways Investments Ltd	Bootle Golf Course	350,000 gallons	9,000 gallons	Other irrigation
Downland Bedding Co Ltd	Blackstock Street	60,000,000 gallons	240,000 gallons	Industrial
Apparelmaster UK Ltd	Mildmay Road, Bootle	94,536,000 litres	363,600 litres	Laundering
British Waterways Board	Leeds & Liverpool Canal	50,000 gallons	0	Standby Emergency
Allied Foods Ltd, Nelson's, Aintree	Long Lane, Aintree	7,200,000 gallons	24,000 gallons	Cooling
Central Edible Oils Co	Dunnings Bridge Road – 2 boreholes	350,000,000 gallons	960,000 gallons	Manufacturing
Walton Hospital	Rice Lane	40,150,000 gallons	110,000 gallons	Washing purposes
Pioneer Concrete (UK) Ltd	Hartley's Village	20,000,000 litres	90,000 litres	Industrial
Associated British Ports	Garston Docks – 2 boreholes	252,000 gallons	16,800 gallons	Washing purposes
Cain's Brewery	Stanhope Street	43,000,000 gallons	360,000 gallons	Manufacturing
Lee Park Golf Club	Gateacre	13,829,550 litres	92,270 litres	Other irrigation
Great Lakes Fine Chemicals Ltd	Halebank, Widnes	250,000,000 gallons	900,000 gallons	Manufacturing
Cargill PLC	Gladstone Dock – 2 boreholes	18,396,000,000 litres	50,400,000 litres	Industrial
Aintree Race Course	Aintree – 2 boreholes	54,600,000 litres	728,000 litres	Other irrigation
Pioneer Concrete (UK) Ltd	Herculaneum Dock	14,000,000 litres	150,000 litres	Industrial

Water supplies in Liverpool

The early days

While Liverpool was a small town, water was not a problem. In 1625, Liverpool consisted of only seven or eight small streets and the water needs of the few hundred residents could be met from the Fall Well located in the vicinity of St John's Lane. At this time, the water was distributed by carts and attempts to bring water from the Bootle wells later in the century failed. In 1786, an Act of Parliament allowed Liverpool to sink more deep wells and pipes were laid to bring water to people who could afford it. Despite the creation of two private water companies, the Bootle Water Company and the Liverpool and Harrington Water Company, water supplies were still expensive, inadequate and intermittent. This state of affairs was unsatisfactory and Liverpool promoted another Act of Parliament in 1843 to use water from the River Mersey for street cleaning, sewer flushing and fire-fighting. The Green Lane Well was sunk in 1846 specifically for fire fighting and the water was piped to the Kensington Service Reservoir, built in 1857, from where it was distributed to various parts of Liverpool.

By the middle of the nineteenth century, it was clear that groundwater supplies underneath Liverpool were inadequate for the needs of the rapidly-growing city. The Waterworks Clauses Act of 1847 imposed a duty on all local authorities to ensure that adequate supplies of water were made available to the people living within their areas. In the same year, Liverpool promoted its own act, the Liverpool Water Act, which allowed it to look for water outside the city limits. This act also enabled Liverpool to take over the two private water companies which, until then, had supplied Liverpool with most of its water. In addition, Liverpool took over the local sewerage boards and appointed James Newlands as City Engineer.

Rivington and the Great Drought of 1865

To replace groundwater supplies, water had to be brought in from outside the city and surface reservoirs had to be constructed. The first of these surface reservoirs was at Rivington Pike, 30 kilometres to the North-East of Liverpool, at the foot of the Rossendale Hills. The Rivington reservoirs are located on the western flank of the Pennines below Anglezarke Moor near the town of Horwich. They occupy a deep valley cut into impermeable Millstone Grit. The Act of Parliament to undertake the Rivington Dam project was passed in 1847 but the

project was highly controversial. Battles raged between 'Pikists', the supporters of the new reservoir and 'Antipikists', who opposed it. In 1850, the matter was resolved by the celebrated railway engineer George Stevenson and the Rivington project went ahead. Construction was started in 1852 and completed in 1856. In its day it would have been considered a major undertaking.

In August 1857, the first water from Rivington was delivered directly to Green Lane in Liverpool and from there it was piped to consumers. The town of Chorley in North-East Lancashire also received its water from Rivington by drawing water from the Rivington aqueduct. The water flowed down the Rivington aqueduct to Liverpool under gravity, thus saving the expense of pumping water. To control the water pressure and flow, balancing reservoirs were built at Aspull, Montrey and Prescot. The first Rivington water supplies were brown in colour and clean well water was mixed with it to make it more palatable. The filter beds were also completed in 1857 and are located at Horwich near Rivington. They improved the quality of the Rivington water but demand continued to grow so rapidly that the wells had to be retained.

Today, there are 8 impounding reservoirs at Rivington with a total storage of over 4,000 million gallons from a modest catchment of 9,710 acres. The supplies are piped by 44ins cast-iron mains for 17·5 miles to Prescot. Construction of the Prescot Holding Reservoirs was six months late and, as a result, the first water was delivered directly to Green Lane. The Rivington water supplies were meant to replace groundwater supplies but this did not happen.

The vastly-increased water supplies now available needed a better system of distribution and new service reservoirs were built from 1854 onwards. Each local service reservoir contained enough water to supply one district in Liverpool for one or two days.

The growth of Liverpool was so great at this time that demand for water soon outstripped the supply from the main Rivington reservoir, even after a second dam was built. The Great Drought of 1865 led to the reopening of some wells and restrictions on the use of water. By September 1865 the situation was so acute that domestic supplies were reduced to one or two hours per day. At one point, only ten days supply remained at Rivington. The drought had a disastrous impact on trade and health in Liverpool. Public baths and wash houses were closed and epidemics claimed many lives, the situation only being relieved by the autumn rainfall.

Above A wooden waterpipe discovered during building work in Williamson Square in the 1930s. Made from hollowed out trees and manufactured off Vauxhall Road, such pipes were commonly used before the mass-manufacture of metal pipes.

Opposite The Breeze Hill underground service reservoir is a masterpiece in brickwork construction. It is emptied periodically for cleaning and maintenance.

In 1866, action was again taken to increase storage capacity at Rivington. Two new wells were sunk, one at Dudlow Lane and the other at Bootle. Since all these measures proved inadequate, Liverpool's Water Engineer, Mr Duncan (not to be confused with Dr Duncan, Liverpool's first Medical Officer of Health), investigated alternative surface supplies from the Lake District, the Pennines and Wales. These plans were put on hold while the new wells were dug. However, the new wells failed to supply as much water as expected and demand continued to grow. Moreover, the Dudlow well caused the local water table in the Woolton area to fall so much that nearby domestic wells dried up. Many of the residents decided to convert their now dry wells into cess pits and organic effluent appeared in the Dudlow Lane deep well which, as a result, had to stop pumping.

The Vyrnwy Scheme

Following Mr Duncan's investigations and the 1865 drought, Wales was selected as a source of water for Liverpool's rapidly-expanding population. In 1879, the decision was taken to build a dam at Vyrnwy in Central Wales. The necessary Act of Parliament was passed in 1880 and construction began at Vyrnwy in 1881 and the dam was completed in 1888.

The Vyrnwy dam and aqueduct was a much larger scheme than Rivington. A large masonry dam was built across a broad valley. Behind the dam is a lake five miles in length with a capacity of over 13,000 million gallons. The reservoir has a catchment area of 23,291 acres, made up of impermeable Ordovician shales. The aqueduct or pipeline to bring the water to Liverpool was a major feat of engineering and took the form of cast-iron underground pipes. It was completed in 1892 with the construction of the 'Mersey Tunnels'.

There are two other large tunnels between Lake Vyrnwy and the filter beds at Oswestry, where the water is passed through layers of sand to filter out solids and chlorine is added to kill bacteria (a practice first used in Liverpool in about 1900). The filter beds now include an ozone plant for disinfecting the water. The water travels to Merseyside by gravity but the pressures generated necessitated the construction of balancing reservoirs or 'break pressure tanks' along the way at Parc Uchaf, Malpas, Cotebrook and Norton. Three 42ins pipelines take the water from Vyrnwy to Runcorn.

Within the Vyrnwy area, there is also a maze of tunnels which feed water from two neighbouring catchments, those of the Afon Marchnant and the Afon Cownwy. Another tunnel takes water directly to the River

Vyrnwy to maintain a steady flow in the river all year round. The main tunnels, the Hirnant and the Aber, feed water to the Vyrnwy aqueduct.

The Great Drought of 1885-8

Before the Vyrnwy scheme was complete, another great drought struck Liverpool in 1884 causing problems similar to those experienced previously. Supplies of water were reduced and a hose-pipe ban was imposed (sounds familiar?). Instead of closing the public baths, saline water was pumped from the new railway tunnel at George's Dock and piped to the baths at Cornwallis Street, Burroughs Gardens and Westminster Road in Central Liverpool. Salt water was also used for street sprinkling and sewer flushing. New deep wells were sunk at Dudlow Lane and Windsor Street in 1888. The Rivington reservoirs reached perilously low levels again in 1885 and 1888. The crisis was such that in July 1891, 12ins steel pipes were laid across the bed of the River Mersey to bring Lake Vyrnwy water to Liverpool, one year before the main Mersey Tunnel pipeline was completed. In March 1892, 12ins cast-iron pipes were temporarily laid in the new Mersey Tunnel before the larger pipes could be installed. The completed Vyrnwy scheme was formally opened in July 1892 and, as the Bootle well water was becoming hard, it was finally closed.

Water from the River Dee

The River Dee has also been exploited as a source of water for Liverpool and the river itself performs the same function as the Vyrnwy Aqueduct in conveying water to the urban areas of the North-West. The headwaters of the River Dee contain a series of lakes in which water is stored to regulate the flow of the river so that a steady supply of water can be abstracted downstream. These lakes include:

- Llyn Tegid (Lake Bala) located on the River Dee itself which was originally built to supply water to the town of Birkenhead. The sluices at Bala were built in 1956 to control the outflow from the lake.
- Llyn Brenig on the Afon Alwen was another Birkenhead project and the dam and aqueduct were completed in 1921.
- Llyn Celyn on the Afon Tryweryn was commissioned by Liverpool Corporation and completed in 1965.

Water from the River Dee is abstracted at Huntington near Chester just above the tidal limit of the River Dee. The water is taken to a treatment works at Huntington and is then sent along two pipelines (with

Water fountains were a common feature of Victorian Liverpool.

diameters of 60 and 72ins) to Norton Water Tower in Runcorn where it joins the Vyrnwy water).

Wallasey purchased water from Liverpool for several decades beginning in the 1920s. The pipeline up the Wirral Peninsula was a novel design in which the pipes were joined by a method called 'turned and bored'. This technique of joining pipes did not work very well and the pipeline leaked badly. Later, Wallasey obtained its water from Birkenhead.

The Mersey Tunnels

At Norton in Runcorn there is a prominent water tower from where the water crosses the Mersey through a pair of tunnels. Here the 'Mersey Tunnels' descend vertically for 60ft and then travel horizontally under the Manchester Ship Canal and the Mersey. The 1892 tunnel used to contain three 42ins water pipelines carrying the Vyrnwy water and the 1938 tunnel contained two 36ins pipes carrying the Dee water. Between the Manchester Ship Canal and the river Mersey, there was a central vertical shaft. On the Lancashire side of the River Mersey, the tunnels and pipelines rise vertically and cross the marshes near Fiddler's Ferry Power Station on their way to Prescot Holding Reservoirs.

The first pipe was laid under the Mersey in 1892 and a second pipe followed in 1905. When the third pipe was laid in 1938, it caused a problem. The tunnel under the canal had a diameter of 3,658mm which was large enough for three pipes, but the tunnel under the river was only 2,748mm and could not take all three pipes. In 1938, a second tunnel was therefore built under the River Mersey for the third Vyrnwy pipe. This proved useful when the Dee water pipes were laid in the tunnels in the 1960s. The second tunnel had to be extended under the canal in 1964 in order to accommodate the new Dee pipelines. These smaller 36 and 42ins pipelines have now been removed and the tunnels refurbished. The tunnels have been relined with welded steel pipes so that each is a pipe in itself. The tunnels under the canal and Mersey have now been joined up underground and the third Vyrnwy pipe which used to 'dog leg' in 'no man's land' from the 1892 Canal tunnel to the 1938 Mersey tunnel has now been abandoned.

The construction of the first Mersey Tunnel under the Manchester Ship Canal was carried out at the same time as the cutting of the canal itself and an open cut was made in the bed of the canal in which the Vyrnwy water pipe could be laid. A massive 3,658mm brick-lined tunnel was built across the bed of the canal to take this pipe. In 1892, the engineers wanted to dredge a path across the bed of the River Mersey but they were not allowed to do this by the Board of Trade and the Mersey Tunnel had to be bored in 'difficult ground' and lined with cast-iron plates, bolted together. This was so difficult that the contractors failed to complete the task and Liverpool City Council employees completed the work under the direction of Mr Deacon, the City Engineer. Timber piles were used to carry the massive pipes in the unsound ground. The underground tunnel link between the Manchester Ship Canal and tunnels under the River Mersey was dug by freezing the ground using sub-zero brine. Liquid nitrogen was used at one point to speed up the freezing process, as brine takes three weeks to freeze up. The new pipes are carried on re-inforced concrete piles instead of wood. Some consideration was given to abandoning one tunnel but both have been retained so that one can be closed down for repairs.

Prescot Holding Reservoirs

Prescot is a small town about three miles east of Liverpool. Two small holding reservoirs were constructed there in 1857 to receive water from the Rivington reservoirs. These holding reservoirs could store enough water to supply Liverpool for a few days. At Prescot, the Vyrnwy water was added to the old Rivington water supply and from here, the water is piped to Liverpool.

At Prescot four smaller storage reservoirs were able to hold 200 million gallons of water, enough water for four days water supply for the Liverpool area. Only two of the four reservoirs are still in use. A new underground reservoir has recently been completed. This underground reservoir was begun in 1979 and will hold 50 million gallons of water. The concrete roof of the underground reservoir is supported by concrete pillars and, being underground, pollution is considerably reduced. At Prescot, the Rivington water was added to the main Vyrnwy supply. Today, so much water from Rivington is drawn off for use in the towns along the Rivington Aqueduct, that the flow is now reversed and Vyrnwy water is used to supply towns in Central Lancashire. The reversed flow needed a different pipe as greater pressures were generated with the pumping of water back up the pipeline. A new Rivington aqueduct was laid in 1996 and this had to take a different route from the old Rivington Aqueduct as much of the area around the old aquaduct has now been built over with houses.

The Water Mains Network

The water distribution network in Liverpool starts with massive cast-iron pipes (the Rivington and Vyrnwy Aqueducts) which bring the treated reservoir water to the Prescot Holding Reservoirs. From Prescot, a series of massive cast-iron pipes called water mains spread out over the Merseyside area. Two pipes run north to North Liverpool and Kirkby and four large water mains run west into Liverpool. Three of these pipes run along Prescot Road to Green Lane. Another heads south to Huyton and South Liverpool and a separate pipeline leaves the Vyrnwy Aqueduct at Cuerdley and leads into Speke.

Local Service Reservoirs

Local service reservoirs were constructed to provide a short term supply and a 'head'. They were usually built in elevated locations so that the water could flow downhill under gravity thus creating water pressure in the taps and saving the cost of pumping. Parts of Liverpool with a lower elevation would have a higher pressure. Places like Woolton and Aubrey Street at higher elevations would be at a disadvantage and water towers were built to supply them.

The old service reservoirs were reminiscent of old Roman cisterns. Some were covered, some were not and most were sunk into the ground. Masonry walls, several feet thick, were constructed from sandstone and the walls and floor were lined with about 6ins of bitumen to provide a watertight seal. Nine inches of brick lined the inside of the bitumen seal. The roof consisted of brick arches, supported by brick pillars. Gravel covered the arches and pipes were laid into it to lead rainwater away. Topsoil covered the gravel and the whole service reservoir was grassed over. The earth dug from the floor was banked up against the stone walls to provide additional support as the water pressure on the walls was enormous. Vents in the roof allowed air to escape.

Inevitably, with the passage of time, the seals would break and the walls would leak. At this point the decision had to be made to either renew or abandon the reservoir.

By 1900, the present pattern of water supply and distribution was established. The main developments in the twentieth century were the construction of the dams on the River Dee. One of the most significant changes, however, was the formation of the North West Water Authority.

There are eight local service reservoirs in Liverpool. Some of these are no longer used and others have been renewed.

Local Service Reservoirs in Liverpool

Reservoir	Date	Status	NB
Aubrey Street	1854	Renewed 1980. Old reservoir filled in	Now made of concrete. Includes a water tower (now a listed building).The old reservoir is now a recreation area. Pumps are needed to raise water to the water tower.
Breeze Hill	1897	Abandoned but intact	It is likely that this site will be donated by North West Water for public open space and will be landscaped using National Lottery money.
Dudlow Lane	1964	Originally built of concrete	Associated with a deep well which is now disused. Its future is uncertain.
High Park Street (Park Hill)	1853	An old sandstone reservoir which leaks	This is the oldest service reservoir still operating and was fed by the Windsor Street borehole. Its use may soon end.
Kensington	1847 & 1857	Renewed 1975	An old stone/brick structure serving north central Liverpool. Now made of concrete. The old reservoir is a recreation area.
Speke	1938	Still operating	
Torr Street (Atherton Street)	1830s	No longer exists	Last remnant of the old Bootle Water Works. Converted into a walled play area.
Woolton	1864	Active	Sandstone masonry structure associated with a water tower. The highest service reservoir. Built for the Dudlow Lane Well. Pumps are needed in Dudlow Lane and at Lode's Pond in Woolton Village.

As the water leaves the reservoirs, the pressure is very strong and can cause problems. The outlet pipe needs to lie much deeper in the ground than normal water mains. For this reason, there are two Liverpool water mains set in bricklined tunnels, one of which carries an 18in pipeline from Torr Street Reservoir to St Domingo Road and the other carries two 18in pipes from Kensington Reservoir to the Royal Hospital. In the latter case, the tunnel cuts through a ridge of sandstone higher than the reservoir itself. On the whole, water mains set in tunnels are uncommon in Liverpool but one exception is a 15yd tunnel which takes an 18in pipeline under Prescot Road near Old Swan.

Local water networks

The water from service reservoirs flows down to housing estates along water mains of varying size, which then feed into individual households. In most cases, pipes are simply laid in trenches, infilled with soil, beneath roads or pavements.

It is common practice to locate sewers below water mains to prevent contamination. In fact, the location of water pipes and sewers is related more to the flow patterns than to possible contamination. Sewers flow by gravity and need to be deep enough to maintain a head and gradient and the depth will therefore vary. Water mains are pressurised and depend only on the head at the local service reservoir.

Opposite The water tower service reservoir at Reservoir Road, Woolton.

Left below A cross section through a local service reservoir.

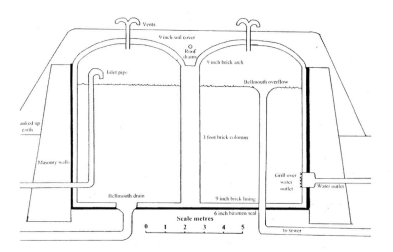

Pipe renewal and replacement

During the nineteenth century, all water pipes were made of cast iron which would slowly corrode and break, so it is not uncommon for water to leak into the sewers. If the flow were reversed and the sewers leaked into the water mains, there could be a serious pollution problem. In November 1995, The Times newspaper reported that this was, in fact, the case but, in May 1996, the paper withdrew the claim and apologised to North West Water. An undisclosed sum of money was donated by the Times to Water Aid.

To avoid sewage contamination, it is essential to maintain the pressure in the water mains. This will, by itself, prevent the ingress of polluted water. In winter, heavy frost cracks pipes and leakage increases. Domestic pipe bursts create an artificially high demand as water flows freely out of the system and the pressure in the area falls. How can this be prevented? One solution is to line the inside of the pipe with a cement wash. To do this, the debris which has accumulated over the years has to be scraped away and the pipe cleaned. A small pipe is then dragged through the water main and a fine spray of cement is used to coat and seal the walls. This does tend to raise the alkalinity of the water and, as the scraper is dragged along the pipe, the branch pipes to individual households are often disturbed, causing further leaks. This technique is used on pipes over 3ins in diameter. Pipes of several feet in diameter are treated with a 'trowler' which is drawn through to spread out the cement. This is a relatively cheap way of renovating old pipes but replacement of the whole pipe is now the favoured option.

Plastic is the preferred alternative to cast iron, as plastic pipes do not corrode or contaminate the water. Digging up the pipe is one method of replacement but there is a simpler way using a cable. The engineers simply drag a machine through the old cast-iron pipe which smashes it. This is called 'pipe drawing' or 'pipe bursting'. The machine which smashes the pipe can be likened to a pneumatic drill. A thin-walled plastic lining tube is drawn through the broken pipe after the drill. A thicker plastic tube with 10mm thick walls is drawn through the thin one. This thicker, more durable tube is sterilised first and set into the ground in sections which are then welded together.

Larger pipes can be treated in a similar way but without breaking the larger, cast-iron pipe. North West Water has pioneered a system of drawing a plastic pipe through the old 40in main. To do this, the old cast iron pipe is cleaned and the plastic pipe compressed in a roller and drawn through it. Once the new plastic pipe is in place, it naturally expands and fits snugly inside the old pipe. This is a very effective but very costly technique (it costs £1 million per mile to line a large pipe). North West Water refurbishes about 450 kilometres of mains each year but with a total of about 40,000 kilometres of water mains in the area, there is a lot of work to do.

These changes are to improve water quality rather than stop mains leakage. Old domestic properties often have lead pipes which can give rise to high lead levels in the water. North West Water regularly tests the water quality all over its network and if the lead content rises above 40 parts per million, the pipes are changed. Plastic connection pipes are laid and new brass taps are set into the street removing the need for a large square 'T' key to shut off the supply to individual properties. Pipes are flushed weekly or monthly and the fire brigade tests flows and purges fire hydrants regularly.

Today, the network is controlled by computer and every house in the area has an individual computer record. All this technology cannot compensate for an ageing water mains network or for people on low incomes who cannot afford the cost of water. Each year some customers who do not pay their bills may have their water supplies cut off. These cut-off notices can only be served with a court order signed by magistrates and both North West Water and the magistrates are reluctant to disconnect young families. Instead of disconnection, payment meters are offered to make payment easier for low-income customers.

Metering may well be a fact of life in the future as the demand for water continues to grow and water supplies become increasingly scarce. However, North West Water is reluctant to introduce metering for all customers. Despite a falling population, demand for water continues to grow. This is partly because a smaller population does not necessarily mean less households and partly as a result of the increasing use of automatic washing machines and dish-washers. Today, the average person consumes about 26 gallons of water per day. Is this rate sustainable? The future may well lie in recycling water. This is happening in the South-East of England but in the North-West, the only recycling practised is where the water from the River Dee, drawn off at Huntington, may have been used by customers upstream. North West Water is doing all it can to reduce leakage but it will remain a serious problem for the foreseeable future.

This collapsed water main in Prescot Road,
Knotty Ash caused a serious flood in 1996.

Sewers and sewage in Liverpool

Cities produce a lot of waste which includes sewage and liquid effluent. Liquid effluent contains relatively clean rainwater or storm drainage and foul waste from toilets, sinks and industrial processes. In suburban areas, foul waste and storm drainage are kept separate where possible but in older, urban areas, they often use the same sewer, known as a combined sewer system. The quantity of the foul waste has increased dramatically over the last 200 years. Two hundred years ago, toilets consisted of latrines with cesspits or privies. In urban areas, the contents of these privies were collected by 'nightsoil' collectors. Gladstone described how the contents of privies were often dumped in the streets, which, being poorly lit, presented an unwelcome hazard to the passer-by. The unenviable job of emptying these privies was often carried out, free of charge, by local farmers who wanted their contents for fertilizer. Carts would travel around the streets of Liverpool and waste would be emptied into them. This would then be transferred to barges which conveyed it to farms along the Leeds – Liverpool Canal. Waste washing water would be cast into the gutter which was, in effect, an open sewer. Waste from the gutters and privies would seep into unpaved streets and into poorly constructed water pipes with inevitable consequences.

The courts would normally share toilets; ratios of ten households to one toilet were not uncommon. At this time, families were large and one can imagine the problems which arose when residents were 'caught short'. The streets shown in the 1891 map of the Beaufort Street area had some large houses with their own outside toilet. Courts number 1, 2, 3 and 4, by contrast, appear to have only two toilets shared between ten houses. The arrangement of steps in court 4 suggests that there is a basement dwelling and court houses with three storeys above ground were not uncommon. A simple calculation might give a possible 20 dwellings in court 4 with each housing a modest family of 5, giving a ratio of 50 residents per toilet!

The advent of the water closet improved things a little but water restrictions were common and particularly acute in the great droughts of the 1860s and 1880s. High water charges and an intermittent water supply, discouraged the spread of water closets, despite the fact that the town and the medical authorities were keen to see their widespread adoption. Under the 1854 Sanitary Amendment Act, Liverpool was given the power to compel residents and landlords to convert their pail closets to water closets. The conversion programme began in 1863 whilst other cities, such as Manchester, were opting for the pail closet

system. Unfortunately, the early sewers were only built to take rainwater and the transport of solids needed a change in design from a box shape to an 'egg' or 'ovoid' shape. Up to 1850, houses with water closets and baths had additional water charges imposed but these were abolished in 1850 to encourage the adoption of the water closets. This only served to increase the demand on an already overstretched water supply. The great drought of 1863-65 must have led some individuals to question whether there would ever be enough water to cater for the widespread adoption of the water closet but the old privies disappeared in the 1890s.

The early sewers

Before sewers were built, natural streams provided the only source of effluent disposal. The Pool was the main drain for Liverpool itself and pollution was a problem even in 1700 and fines were imposed on the trades and individuals who polluted it. Natural streams such as Tue or Tew Brook lay outside the Liverpool town limits until the end of the Nineteenth Century. These streams could possibly cope with sewage for a small rural community but not with that of a rapidly-growing urban population. Though many of the streams are now culverted, the sewer network does resemble the old stream pattern.

Inadequate sanitation led to high levels of illness in Liverpool and periodic epidemics of fatal diseases such as cholera and typhoid occurred throughout the Nineteenth Century. Daymond describes how cholera first came to Liverpool from India in May 1832 when sixteen hundred people died. Liverpool had limited powers of drainage and sewerage and stronger powers were needed if the epidemics were to be eliminated. Liverpool's problems were particularly pressing, as rapid population growth, particularly after 1840, led to severe overcrowding. Daymond states that between 16 January and 17 May 1847, 128,000 Irish people came to Liverpool, following the potato famine. In 1840, Dr Duncan, not yet in place as Medical Officer for Health, produced a report highly critical of the state of Liverpool's sewers. In 1842 an Act of Parliament was passed which enabled the city to upgrade them. It also transferred the task of sewerage from the old Commissioners to the Liverpool town council. From this point on, co-ordination was possible and a comprehensive sewer network could evolve.

Rapid house construction took place during the mid-nineteenth century but this provided very basic accommodation. Large families and

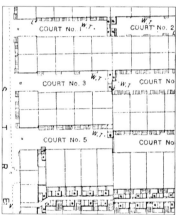

Above top A street sprinkling cart at the the turn of the century. Surface wash from the streets would run into the sewers.

Above A map detail showing the distribution of toilets and water taps in one of Liverpool's many congested slums.

Opposite Liverpool's rapidly growing population was marked by a housing boom and the expansion of sewers to keep pace with this was becoming difficult. Many court residents had to share toilets in the 'good old days'.

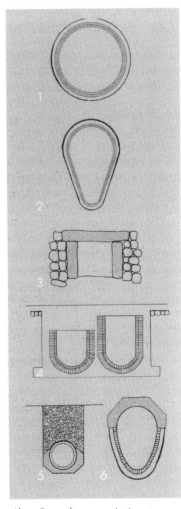

Above Types of sewers and culverts in Liverpool: 1, Northern outfall sewer; 2, egg shaped brick ovoid, the most common type of sewer; 3, old stone lined stream culvert; 4, double storm culvert, used only in the Pier Head area; 5, The modern construction method of a concrete or clay pipe laid in a trench; 6, post-war egg shaped sewer.

multiple occupation of dwellings produced the inevitable slums, with poverty an ever-present phenomenon. Cholera epidemics broke out in 1832, 1849, 1854 and 1866 and, in 1848, a series of other epidemics occurred. In 1847, the death rate in the slums was 1 in 7, whilst in more affluent areas it was only 1 in 28. It was now appreciated that dirty water was a major cause of ill health. In 1802, a bill to improve Liverpool's sanitation failed due to vested interests. However, between 1830 and 1840, 20 miles of sewers were built but by 1846, there were still only 56 miles of sewers in a town with a population of 251,000 people. There were seven outfalls to the river and these drained only half of Liverpool's eight square mile area.

The 'Sanatory Act' (sic) of 1846 provided the framework for improving sewers and drainage systems, the paving of roads and various sanitary improvements in Liverpool. Perhaps more significantly, the city appointed its first Medical Officer of Health, Dr Duncan. The following year, 1847, when the act actually came into force, James Newlands was appointed City Engineer. His sewer construction programme began in 1848 and, during the next eleven years, 86 miles of new sewers were built. Although epidemics did not cease, they became less frequent and less devastating. Another 58 miles of sewers were built between 1856 and 1862. Clean water was now being piped in increasing quantities from Rivington Pike and, after 1858, most new houses were provided with water closets rather than pail privies. Water shortages, however, continued to thwart sanitary improvements and it would take many years to eradicate the legacy of past indifference and neglect. Ironically, the decline in epidemic, water-borne illness predated the discovery of their cause. The link between clean water and disease was appreciated but poorly understood; during years in which cholera epidemics broke out, long queues formed at public baths. Newland's sewer programme was completed in 1869.

The early sewer network

During the Eighteenth Century, crude sewers were built which ran under gravity down to the River Mersey. Beacon Gutter, designed by John Rennie in 1813, was one of the earliest sewers, although it was not built until 1830. It was a brick-lined structure with a lime mortar, cut into sandy clay and chemical waste. This chemical waste was so caustic, that it rotted the boots and clothes of the navvies constructing the sewer and gave off poisonous fumes. The dimensions of the sewer

started with a 5ft by 3ft 8ins ovoid, increasing at the outfall to 6ft by 4ft 6ins. It is usual for sewers to increase in size as they get nearer the outfall to accommodate the increasing flows. Sometimes this happens gradually and, in other sewers, there is a sudden change in diameter.

Another example of an early sewer was the Kirkdale Outfall. Interceptor sewers were built at right-angles to this outfall and ran along the east and west side of the main ridges such as that at Everton. These were called the Everton Relieving Sewers.

On the south side of the city, Mosslake was drained by a sewer whose outfall was in Dingle Lane. The Dingle Lane outfall was built in 1849 and was cut into solid sandstone with an average depth of 29ft. Larger sewers tend to be deeper. Sewers are generally classified according to size and depth.

A sewer ran down Paradise Street along the line of the old Pool into George's Dock. Heavy rain would cause this sewer to overflow which caused flooding. A relief sewer, 5ft 6ins by 4ft was built for storm water between 1859 and 1861. Diversions past George's Dock were completed on the south side in 1861 and the north side in 1862.

Some of these sewers emptied straight into the docks; in these cases, the co-operation of the Dock Board was needed and, in some instances, the Dock Board helped with the cost of construction. Lord Derby also assisted with finance for the construction of sewers, as he had substantial business interests in the Vulcan Street area. Most of these sewers are now disused.

Sewer construction

Liverpool's sewers had numerous different designs depending on when and where they were built. The early sewers which carried only rainwater were simply enclosures of streams. The transport of solids needed a narrower channel so that even in low flow, the 'invert' or bottom of the sewer could maintain a reasonably rapid flow. If this did not happen, the solids would build up. The sewers were constructed and lined with brick. The brick lining provided strength, protection from aggressive groundwater and occasionally helped to improve the flow of the sewage. Cleansing is best achieved by having a strong flow and this is achieved by having a steep gradient with a minimum gradient of 1 in 40, common for small house drains. As the size of the sewer increases, so does the velocity of the flow. Thus for a larger sewer, a gradient of 1 in 1000 can achieve a good self-cleansing flow regime.

Sewers frequently ran under main roads which often meant construction and repair caused traffic chaos even before the car era. The Northern Outfall shown here under construction in Regent Road was photographed in November 1913.

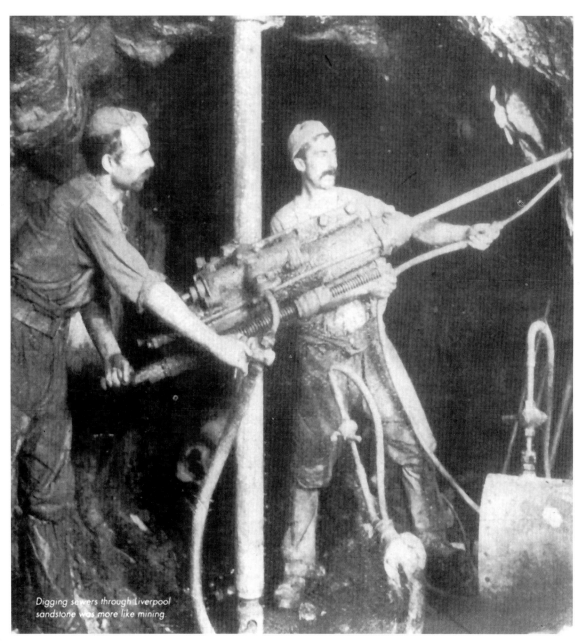

Digging sewers through Liverpool sandstone was more like mining.

The sewers were sometimes tunnelled in sandstone and some of these tended to be relatively deep underground. Rock-cut sewers are relatively uncommon now but were more common in relatively high areas such as Toxteth where the sandstone is near the surface. The Toxteth sewer had the invert lined with radiating blue brick and the sides were concreted. Sewers cut into the surface tended to remain near the surface, although Lord Derby's Brunswick Place sewer built in 1864 averaged a depth of 26ft and, at one point, it reached a depth of 59ft. This, like many other sewers, was cut into poor ground, made up of sand and clay and it collapsed in 1887, having developed bulges. It ended up being lined with cast-iron piping, although this had to be significantly smaller than the sewer which had become deformed in the unstable ground. The Paradise Street sewers were built in the mud of the Pool. Poor ground is still a problem today despite concrete pipes and mechanical diggers. The Windbourne outfall extension was constructed to facilitate the construction of the river wall at Otterspool. Within a few years, it suffered settlement and cracking and had to be replaced on piled foundations.

Occasionally, sewers had to be cut into old debris and rubble. The problems of cutting in old chemical waste are mentioned above. The mortar lining was always subject to corrosion by the infiltration of groundwater but corrosion was increased where the sewer was laid in chemical waste. In the Dingle, one of the old dingles was called Dickinson's Dingle. The waste sandstone from the Brunswick Railway Tunnel was disposed of in this dingle. Since sewers often follow the lines of old drainage channels, they cut the New Dingle sewer into this old railway tunnel rubble which was not an easy task.

One critical factor in construction was that the materials and methods used should be of the highest standard and quality. Since sewer construction work in James Newlands' day was all put out to contract, as it is today, strict supervision was needed to avoid errors and bad practice. Some of the failures which arose were due to poor work. In 1866, the brick-lined sewers in the Great Homer Street, Stanley Road and Sandhills area appeared to be sound. In fact, the contractors had cut away more rock than was needed and had not back-filled properly between the brick lining and the rock tunnel. When the tide rose and restricted the sewer outflow, great pressure built up from storm water and the sewer burst. It was then found that the 9ins brick lining was actually only 4ins. In 1879, Liverpool Corporation stopped using contractors and organised its own construction team.

Sewer construction in open country was cheap. Construction costs in open country were only 15 shillings per yard during these early days. Unfortunately, urban growth outpaced sewer construction. The construction of some sewers was planned for open countryside but, by the time sewers were in fact built, these areas had already become built-up which raised the cost of construction to £2-3 per yard.

Problems of sewers

Many problems arose even where conditions and construction methods were sound. Sewers designed to take rainwater were not suited to solids. Many sewers were too small in size to cope with the increasing needs of the rapidly-growing population and house construction exceeded both the capacity of the sewers and the water supplies. The water supply problem was not solved until the Lake Vyrnwy Scheme and the Vyrnwy Aqueduct were completed at the end of the century. In the Everton area, house construction also increased runoff due to the paving over of the land surface. This increased the flow into the sewers during periods of heavy rain. The rapid conversion of privies to water closets also increased the discharge into the sewers.

Slack flow due to insufficient gradient was exacerbated by water shortages which were particularly acute in the 1860s and 1880s. Today there is plenty of water and the flows are normally adequate. There is one exception: the Paradise Street sewers were built for domestic use when many people lived in the town centre. Few people live in this area today and low flow volumes sometimes lead to a build up of solids and smells.

The dynamics of flow were poorly understood in the middle of the nineteenth century and junctions between side and main sewers were made at right-angles. It was soon realised that if two sewers met at an acute angle, the flow would be much better. At first, side sewers were joined to the main sewer at invert level but this was changed and now side sewers enter the main sewer at springer level. Some side sewers even enter at the top of the main sewer, i.e. soffit level; this is now the preferred type of junction. Anyone who has seen domestic sewers being laid, will appreciate that there are set junction pipes with fixed angles.

Collapsing sewers are still a problem. In the 'new' sewer network built during the nineteenth century, collapsing sewers were uncommon. However, when it occurred, the collapse could be spectacular. In

Grouting the sewer wall under Ullet Road in 1927.

Above Venting is a minor problem today, as most houses have a sewer venting system with a soil pipe projecting above the eaves of the roof. There are, however, a few sewer vents still around.

Right A diagrammatic section through the storm chambers where old sewers are intercepted by the MEPAS – The Merseyside Estuary Pollution Alleviation Scheme or interceptor sewer.

Opposite left Working in a brick ovoid sewer, five feet by three feet, could be a demanding experience.

Opposite right A worker in the four feet by two feet Orwell Road/Juniper Street sewer, where work was cramped and uncomfortable.

1866, the Boundary Street section of the Beacon Gutter sewer collapsed between Vauxhall Road and the Leeds/Liverpool canal. The alarm was first raised when the ground started to sink. Due to the proximity of the Leeds/Liverpool canal and the railway, the bridges on both were undermined and it took seven months to repair the damage. Today, the need for repairs is just as common and rebuilding is sometimes necessary. A new method of repairing sewers uses a polypropylene resin. The damaged sewer has an inflated tube inserted into the damaged section and resin is injected between the sewer wall and the inflated tube. The resin sets almost immediately, sealing and strengthening the sewer. Sewers can also be replaced by 'pipe bursting' or 'pipe jacking' in which a wedge is dragged through the sewer to smash it and a new plastic sewer is drawn through behind. This is similar to the method described in the previous chapter, where it is used to renew water pipes.

Sometimes the sewers were too small for the storm overflow. In the Brunswick Street/Oil Street area there are warehouses whose floors were on a level with the sewer invert and were flooded when the sewage overflowed.

During the 1975-77 drought, the slack flow caused sewage build-up in the sewer and the smell matched the old pre-sewer days. Sewers need proper ventilation which was sometimes provided by vertical, 6ins cast-iron pipes erected over them. At the base of the pipe was a chamber containing charcoal which was meant to absorb noxious gasses. This was deemed to be unsuccessful and they were replaced by grids. Venting is a minor problem today, as most houses have a sewer venting system with a soil pipe projecting above the eaves of the roof. There are, however, a few sewer vents still around. Smells do occasionally occur, as in Paradise Street, but this is rare.

In areas like Whitechapel and Paradise Street which are low lying, it is difficult to provide effective drainage. Thunderstorms and heavy rains can make the sewers overflow and houses have, on occasion, been flooded, which causes understandable distress. In 1789, one such flood necessitated the Liverpool Infirmary fitting out a vacant ward as a temporary residence for flood displaced families.

The rapid growth of Liverpool during the nineteenth century meant that the old systems could not cope. Because of this, a storm water culvert in Whitechapel and Paradise Street was built to take excess rainwater.

Design of the sewers

The earliest sewers were rectangular, not unlike the old Roman sewers under York. This design is still used for culverts but they are now constructed from reinforced concrete. A similar design and was used for the Central storm water culverts over the short length from Water Street via the Pier Head to the river.

Egg-shaped sewers, with a narrow invert, were intended to provide an efficient flow regime and a strong structural design. These are described as 'brick ovoids' and are commonly 3ft tall by 1ft 10ins wide – not a lot of room to work in!. They were normally lined with brick but there are exceptions. A section of a sewer along Sefton Street (the Dock Road) from Parliament Street to Park Street used to be unlined until the early 1980s. Beacon Gutter, built in 1848, was a small ovoid, while the town centre sewers of Whitechapel and Castle Street are slightly larger. When sewers collapse, the soffit is replaced with a pre-cast concrete cap.

Today, circular sewers are the norm. The 8ft main Northern Outfall Sewer is one of the city's largest. Concrete and clay pipes have replaced many of the old brick sewers. They are now laid in trenches and usually back-filled with granular materials. Main sewers are nearly always situated under the highway.

At the sewer outfall into the river, there were problems with the tides. Teak valves called 'tide' or 'flap' valves were installed at each outfall to stop the tide flowing back up the sewers. When worn out, they were replaced with heavy, cast-iron valves. These outfall valves are even more important today, as they prevent the ingress of river water into the new MEPAS or Interceptor Sewer. Smaller branch sewers had their own

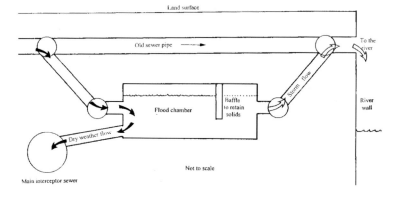

Above The Northern Outfall eight feet wide sewer in 1922.

Right A map of the sewer works of Liverpool and th MEPAS scheme.

Opposite The steel lined ovoid sewer in Rice Lane may be cleaner but it is still cramped.

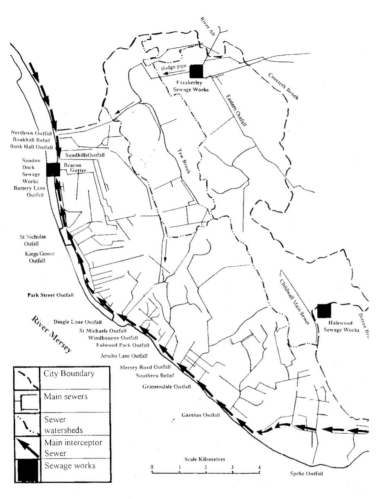

smaller teak valves and many city centre shops and businesses also have their own flap valves. This necessarily meant that for a few hours on each tide, outflow from the sewers was impossible and sewage had to be stored in the sewer. Some outfalls had narrower outlets to make the outflow faster and more effective, producing a scouring effect. In 1993, a spectacular accident occurred when a 25 ton crane was raising a two metre square, cast-iron flap valve in Gower Street. As seven sewer men were entering the sewer, the flap fell and trapped the legs of three of them. This was unusual, as safety is now a big issue, unlike 100 years ago.

The modern sewer network

The Northern Outfall Sewer is the largest and deepest sewer in Liverpool. Its construction was authorised by the city's Health Committee in 1913 but construction was stopped during the First World War. It was completed in 1925 and then extended in 1931. This sewer is unique in that it breaches a watershed. Pumping is normally required to lift sewage over a watershed and there are 18 pumping stations scattered around the city today. The Northern Outfall Sewer drains the central plateau of Liverpool, which was formerly drained by Tue Brook. It was built to avoid overloading the Fazakerley Sewage Works following the rapid expansion of Liverpool's urban area. It is a large 8ft sewer, widening to 9ft for the last 1,000yds (it is possible to sail along this sewer in a dinghy). It used to discharge into the Canada Basin, but was modified earlier this century and, in 1989, was intercepted as part of MEPAS. Liverpool's sewers used to discharge straight into the River Mersey.

The Southern Relief Sewer was also planned before the First World War but construction was also held up and not completed until 1924 and, like the northern sewers, this sewer bears some relation to existing stream patterns. Three feeder sewers from Thingwall Road, Penny Lane and Booker Avenue converge to make one large sewer 8ft x 5ft 4ins, which used to discharge into the Mersey at Otterspool.

The Speke Outfall was the last combined outfall sewer to be built because Speke was the last area to be incorporated into Liverpool and one of the last areas to be built up. In the early days, a small 3ft x 2ft sewer drained a rural area of farms and cottages around the village of Speke. Farms tended to have their own drains and soakaways and therefore a large sewer was not necessary. The construction of Liverpool Airport between the wars necessitated proper sewering. A new sewer was built in the 1930s and the old one abandoned. This new sewer starts as a 21-inch sewer and increases to 5ft 9ins by 3ft 10ins. It then emptied into the river as the Speke Outfall but has now recently been intercepted. Two important branches to this sewer from Dungeon Lane and Oglet Lane used to join the Speke Outfall on the Mersey foreshore.

The Eastern Outfall Sewer drains the West Derby and Dovecot areas. There is a 4ft by 2ft 8ins sewer in Finch Lane and two 36-inch sewers in King's Drive and Dovecot Avenue. A relief sewer was built in Croxteth Hall Lane. These all feed into the Fazakerley Sewage Treatment Works.

Childwall Valley was developed for housing somewhat later than other areas. Construction of a sewer was agreed in 1930 because the old Woolton sewers were inadequate for the rapid urban growth. The Childwall Valley Sewer runs down towards Netherley where it needs pumping to the Halewood Sewage Works. This sewer starts off as a 9-inch pipe in Score Lane and increases to a 36-inch concrete pipe as it approaches the sewage works.

By 1938, there were 19 separate outfalls between the Bootle boundary to the north to the Speke suburbs on the south. The city had grown by stages since 1835. There were still many sewers running straight down to the to the river. In fact the layout in 1938 was not so different from that of today. The construction of the Otterspool Promenade merely required the extension of the sewers out underneath the reclaimed land where they then discharged straight into the river as before. Today, only storm water discharges straight into the river.

Local sewage works

The inland plateaux had a system of sewers running along the line of the old streams. These ran to the Fazakerley Sewage Treatment Plant. This received the sewers from both the Tuebrook and the Alt valleys. Here the sewage was treated by settlement and biological degradation, which is described as primary and secondary treatment. The waste water is discharged into the River Alt and the sludge pumped over to the Northern Outfall Sewer. A smaller sewage works was located nearby on Back Gillmoss Lane but this has now been abandoned.

Halewood Sewage Works receives sewers from the Childwall Valley area and discharges effluent into the Ditton Brook after primary and secondary treatment.

Opposite left The Aigburth Vale Relief Sewer is a large concrete lined modern sewer.

Opposite right Drilling the Aigburth Vale Relief Sewer in Mersey Road, photographed in 1985, involved cutting through solid sandstone.

In 1974, Liverpool's sewer system was transferred to North West Water. Like the water supply network, the sewer system never exactly corresponded to the Liverpool boundary and there was the opportunity to create a more integrated network on Merseyside.

The problem

It soon became clear that the River Mersey could not cope with the sewage from the towns and conurbations along its length. Not only did Liverpool, during the 1960s, discharge about 35 million gallons of untreated sewage into the lower Mersey each day, but the upper Mersey received sewage from the Manchester area and numerous towns and industries along its banks. The organic effluent and sewage was broken down by bacteria in the water which in turn used up the dissolved oxygen in the river. By 1980, the oxygen levels at Widnes had fallen to zero. The result was that the lower Mersey was effectively dead. When the oxygen is all used up, little life can be supported and the fish die. The bacteria then stop breaking down the organic matter and river starts to smell. As the Mersey widens into the basin, the river water merges with the sea and the oxygen levels rises again. People fishing off the Seaforth Dock have reported that, at certain stages of the tide, fishing was difficult as their fishing lines became fouled with toilet paper! Something had to be done!

The Mersey Estuary is 50 kilometres long with a tidal limit at Howley Weir at Warrington. Most of the estuary is classed as having a water quality classification of class C or D. C and D class rivers are described as poor or bad. Until recently Liverpool and Wirral had about 28 sewer outfalls along the 23 kilometres of the Mersey shore. Raw sewage could frequently be seen in the river. New Brighton had been eclipsed as a resort and fishing was non-existent in many places. Ironically, London had the same problem and action was taken over a century ago. The solution was the subject of a long debate. There were several options.

One option was to build individual small screening plants on each outfall. Even if there were the sites for these works, the cost would have been prohibitive. Mini interceptor sewers could be built to a series of small sewage treatment plants. This was a more viable option in Wirral.

Expansion of the inland sewage works at Fazakerley and Halewood was considered. If this were done, the Mersey outfalls could be diverted inland. This was feasible but the River Alt and Ditton Brook could not cope with the volume of partially treated sewage. There was even a scheme to treat the sewage at Fazakerley and pump the effluent back to Canada Dock.

Eventually, Sandon Dock became vacant and, after negotiations with the Mersey Docks and Harbour Company, it was agreed a new sewage treatment works could be built on that site. There would be a berth for sludge ships to take the sludge for dumping in the Irish Sea.

Mersey Estuary Pollution Alleviation Scheme (MEPAS)

The interceptor sewer, or MEPAS, runs from Speke in the south and Crosby in the north with the sewage being collected at Sandon Dock. In fact, the southern section starts in Knowsley at a small treatment works on the Halewood/Speke boundary. MEPAS increases in size as it intercepts more and more sewers. It starts off as a 1·2 metre pipeline in Speke and increases to 2·1 metres at Garston, rising to 2·4 metres along the Dock Road. The pipeline runs the full length of the east bank of the Mersey Estuary. The majority of its length had to be tunnelled using a tunnelling machine with only the Speke section using open cut excavation. From Garston right up to Otterspool, the tunnel was cut in surface clays and muds. From Otterspool to the Pier Head, much of the tunnel is cut in rock. The remainder of the distance to Sandon Dock was cut in various sediments. Four pumps are needed along MEPAS, and they are located in Speke and Crosby. The rest of the flow from Garston and Bootle to Sandon Dock is achieved by gravity. At Speke, the interceptor sewer is at 8 metres OD, i.e. 8 metres above sea-level. At Sandon Dock, the sewer is – 8 metres OD, i.e. 8 metres below sea-level. This gives a fall of 16 metres over the full length of the pipeline. When finished, the MEPAS scheme will have cost £280 million. Construction of the Sewer started in 1988 at Sandon Dock. The first 2·2 kilometres of the interceptor sewer nearest the dock will intercept and divert 45% of the entire sewage discharged into the Mersey from the east shore. Very rapid and significant gains were therefore experienced at an early stage.

To connect old sewers to the new interceptor sewer, the interceptor sewer needs to pass deep under the old sewer. At each outfall, a storm water chamber has been built and the old sewer is diverted into this storm chamber. Dry weather flow from the old sewer flows down into the interceptor sewer. If it rains heavily, the surplus water accumulates in the storm chamber and runs into the estuary. When the tank level is

at a pre-set maximum, the floating solids are prevented from discharging with this overflow by a baffle wall that hangs from the roof. Heavy solids accumulate at the bottom of the tank. The discharge from these tanks is very dilute and is strictly limited.

The northern section of the interceptor sewer is ten kilometres long and is now complete. It starts in Crosby and intercepts six outfall sewers. The first 4·5 kilometres of this interceptor sewer needs pumping; the rest of this sewer flows under gravity.

Nineteen sewers had been intercepted by 1997 and the tunnellers had reached Outfall 13 in Jericho Lane by May 1997. The entire 26 kilometre length was completed in August 1997.

Sandon Dock

Work began to reclaim this site in 1984 although the necessary planning permission was given in 1980. The sewage works covers eight hectares and there is room for expansion to 19 hectares. The first operation was to pump out 90,000 cubic metres of river silt which was 2·3 metres deep over the floor of the dock. Over half a million tons of sand, 13 metres deep, was used to fill the dock. By January 1975, this first stage had been completed. The warehouses around the dock were then demolished and construction began. This was completed in 1991 and sewage treatment could begin.

It has been built to handle a normal dry-weather flow of 300 megalitres per day but can cope with a wet-weather flow of 950 megalitres per day. This is the sewage output from the equivalent of one million people but is made up of the sewage from 450,000 people and the equivalent of 550,000 people in industrial effluent. Fazakerley and Halewood can handle 63 megalitres of sewage per day from inland areas. The final cost for the construction of the Sandon Dock Sewage Works was £50 million. There is a clear diurnal pattern of sewage discharge based on the working day of the people of Liverpool: sewage flows are low at night and high during the day.

Treatment

The sewage is transported to the Sandon Dock Sewage Works by the Interceptor running under the dock road. Eight powerful pumps lift the sewage into the screening plants where large objects are screened. This is followed by grit removal and several skips of grit are filled each day. Much of this is washed off the roads of Liverpool. The organic part of the sewage settles out in the long primary settlement tanks. In these tanks, rotating blades scrape the sludge to one end of the tank. From here, it is pumped into the digesters where it produces gas which can be used to heat the digesters; this gas also powers the pumps. At the moment, the digested sludge is shipped out into the Irish Sea to be dumped but this will have to stop in 1998 due to a European Union directive which prohibits the dumping of sludge at sea. The sludge will then be dumped in landfill sites or go for incineration at Fiddlers Ferry. Grit is already being dumped in landfill sites. The whole treatment plant has very few staff and is highly automated with computers controlling all stages of the processing. In the year 2000, it is planned to start secondary treatment.

The sewage works is a subterranean labyrinth in itself. Passages run underneath many of the main tanks and roadways. These are lined with pipes with different colour codes. Computer terminals are installed at various points in these tunnels so that an operative can check what process is going on and how much sewage is passing through the system.

One hundred and fifty years have passed since James Newlands was given the task of planning and constructing sewers for Liverpool. He would be impressed with the achievements which have been made during this time and also appreciate the problems of maintaining a system which evolved over one and a half centuries. Building and maintaining sewers is like painting the Forth Bridge – it never ends!

Railways under Liverpool

The first railway

Liverpool can boast the first fully-operational railway line in the world, the Liverpool and Manchester Line, which was opened on 15 September 1830. George Stephenson, the railway builder, had many problems to face along the route. The relief of the land was relatively flat for much of the way but when the line arrived in Liverpool there were two major obstacles. The Woolton-Broadgreen ridge was steep and a massive cutting was excavated to maintain a reasonable gradient along the line. The Olive Mount cutting, which is half a mile long, 80ft deep and 20ft wide, is still one of the deepest in the world and later railway engineers would have dug a tunnel through a ridge such as this.

Crown Street Tunnel

From Olive Mount, the railway line crosses a plateau on which extensive marshalling yards were built. The next obstacle was the ridge at Edge Hill. The first station at the Liverpool terminus was built at Crown Street which is situated at a higher elevation than the plateau. The trains had to travel up a steeply-inclined tunnel to Crown Street and were drawn up by cables. Similar cables were also needed at the other end of the Liverpool to London line where they were needed to pull the trains from Euston to Camden. The Crown Street tunnel was completed in 1829 and was 290yds long, 15ft wide and 12ft high. A line can still be seen entering the area adjacent to Smithdown Lane. On the return journey, the trains would be lowered down to Edge Hill using the cables.

The Lime Street Tunnel

Crown Street was not used for long because the Lime Street tunnel was was opened on 15 August 1836. This tunnel was 2,230yds long and went downhill at a gradient of 1 in 93. This may not sound steep to motorists but was about three times as steep as the Liverpool to Manchester Railway. In section, this tunnel was 25ft wide and 17ft high. At first, this was a relatively narrow tunnel which could only accommodate two railway lines but, in the 1880s, it was widened to take four tracks and much of the rock over the tunnel was removed making it open to the sky for much of its length. It can now be seen from the surface through these openings, which are surrounded by high walls for safety. There are seven sections of true tunnel along this line.

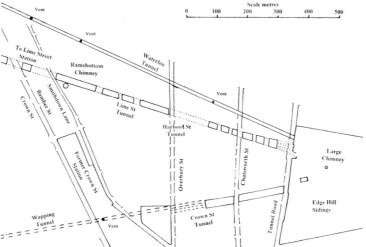

Above Engraving of the construction of the Liverpool/Manchester railway tunnel at Edge Hill.

Opposite The Olive Mount cutting which is half a mile long, eighty feet deep and twenty feet wide is still one of the deepest in the world.

Left The railway tunnels of Central Liverpool.

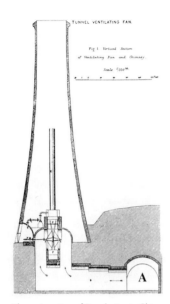

TUNNEL VENTILATING FAN.

Fig.1 Vertical Section of Ventilating Fan and Chimney. Scale 1:200

A

Above A section of Ramsbottom's Chimney, showing where the ventilation fan was placed and the drift from tunnel 'A'.

Right There were several problems associated with the Lime Street Tunnel. When steam locomotives started to use the tunnel, smoke was a major hazard. The solution was a giant, steam-driven fan at Smithdown Lane. This was designed by John Ramsbottom, the Chief Mechanical Engineer for the LNWR and was built in 1870.

- The first tunnel is about 50yds long and lies under aptly named Tunnel Road and Moorgate Street. This tunnel had a double bore in the centre with single bores on either side. Tunnel Road was built to give access to Edge Hill Station.

- The second tunnel runs under Harbord Street for over 100yds.

- The third tunnel, only 20yds long, runs under Mason Street and is little more than a bridge.

- The fourth tunnel of just under 100yds in length, runs under Smithdown Lane.

- The fifth tunnel of 30yds has twin bores and runs under Crown Street.

- The sixth tunnel goes under Brownlow Hill and the University for about 130yds and has twin tunnels each with two tracks. Since the end of steam in 1968, the open cutting between the fifth and sixth tunnels has been raftered over by Liverpool University to improve the environment.

- The seventh tunnel of just over 100yds runs under Russell Street and then opens out onto Lime Street Station platforms.

In addition, there is a single line tunnel labelled as a shunting tunnel, on the north side of the main track which runs east from Lime Street Station and joins up with the main track at Brownlow Street. Initially, trains travelling down this incline had to be 'uncoupled from their locomotives at Edge Hill and the carriages then lowered down to Lime Street Station by cables. At Lime Street, the carriages were marshalled about by teams of horses working in fours. Horses could only cope with lighter carriages and, as they became heavier, locomotives were needed to move them about. This tunnel cost a staggering £150,000 to build.

The mechanism for hauling the trains was described as an 'endless rope' and it was made of hemp. Two engines located beside the track at Edge Hill would haul and lower the carriages down to Lime Street Station. An enormous chimney associated with the winding engine was located at Edge Hill. It was 310ft high and was only demolished in 1937. In March 1870, the engines and ropes were replaced by steam locomotives and the horses were dispensed with altogether.

The opening out of the Lime Street Tunnel

There were several problems associated with the Lime Street Tunnel. When steam locomotives started to use the tunnel, smoke was a major hazard. The solution was a giant, steam-driven fan at Smithdown Lane. This was designed by John Ramsbottom, the Chief Mechanical Engineer for the LNWR and was built in 1870. A tunnel was cut into the sandstone from the railway tunnel. The engine was located in a large, subterranean cavern. Above this was a massive chimney, rising 198ft above rail level. The fan was only used when a train entered the rail tunnel and it took only eight minutes to clear the tunnel. The massive chimney was only demolished in the 1960s. The fan soon became redundant when, in 1881, the Lime Street Tunnel was opened out.

The second problem was that the two original tracks in the tunnel were inadequate for the growth in traffic using Lime Street Station. In 1873, it was decided to increase the lines from two to four. Excavation started at Lime Street Station where the ground under the present Copperas Hill and St Vincent Street was dug out. Few explosives were used because of safety considerations. As the cutting progressed back up the line, the engineers were pleased that little additional support was needed for the vertical rock walls. The railway company wanted to close some streets completely but the council refused and cross streets were carried on brick and stone arches constructed as the cutting was deepened. Where the cutting was deeper, rock arches were left to carry the roads. The sewers, on the other hand, had to be diverted. In the deeper sections of the cutting, the sewers could be carried within the stone arches over the railway. One sewer, however, could not be contained within the stone arch and was carried over the cutting in a cast-iron box as a 'flying sewer'.

Powers were obtained in 1878 to take a four-track line all the way back to Edge Hill, mostly in the form of open cuttings. Tunnels were only excavated where important roads crossed the line. Accidents occurred in 1879 and 1880 in which one locomotive ploughed into the back of the train in front. These accidents were caused by smoke obscuring the driver's view and demonstrated the need for the opening out of the line. The cutting was dug to its full depth on the south side first and the new tunnels were cut before the old tunnel could be exposed.

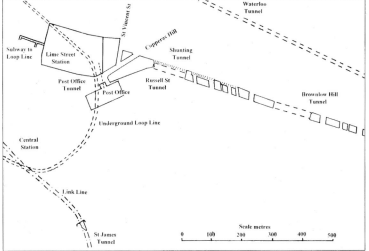

Left The main Lime Street tunnel from Edge Hill enters the Station with the small shunting tunnel on the left.

Below Left The approach to Lime Street Station

A fifth line was built from Lime Street Station to Brownlow Street following an act passed in 1882. This line was built in a separate tunnel to avoid disturbing the new four-track construction and was needed for shunting purposes. The new works were opened in 1885.

The Wapping Tunnel

Construction of the Wapping tunnel commenced in 1827 when a series of vertical shafts were sunk along the line of the proposed tunnel. From these shafts, pilot headings were excavated in both directions until they met other headings from the nearby shafts. This tunnel was designed by George Stephenson and the engineer was Charles Vignoles. Houses near and above the line of the tunnel were threatened with collapse by the tunnelling operations in Great George Square. The line of the tunnel was surveyed by TL Gooch, whose brother worked for the Great Western Railway. The initial survey for the tunnel had serious errors and Joseph Locke submitted a report exposing them and Charles Vignoles resigned. To rectify the errors, side shafts were cut to check alignment and the mistakes were corrected. At its upper end, the Wapping Tunnel uses the same approach as the Crown Street Tunnel and runs parallel to it for about 100yds. The Cheshire Lines tunnel crosses over the Wapping tunnel at Great George Street and is carried on girders. Most of the Wapping Tunnel is cut in sound red sandstone. Where this was not the case, some of it had to be lined with brick to give extra support.

The Wapping tunnel is about 1¼ miles long and for much of its length has a gradient of 1 in 48, very steep for that time. In fact, gradients as steep as 1 in 38 are used at the upper and lower ends of the tunnel. The Wapping tunnel was built to carry goods to the docks and the Wapping Goods Station (known as Park Lane goods station after 1923) was built at the river end of the line opposite the Wapping dock. A report in Fraser's Guide dated 1855 states that at the lower end of the tunnel near Wapping Dock, the tunnel went under dockside warehouses where trap doors in the basements allowed goods to be loaded and unloaded directly onto the trains. The famous Moorish Arches at Edge Hill were built to house the engines that worked the cables. As at Lime Street, these cables hauled the wagons up and down the incline of the tunnel on an 'endless rope' system. Six wagons, with an average weight of 4 tons, could be hauled at any one time giving a total load of 27 tons. When stronger steel cables replaced hemp, sixteen wagons could be hauled at one time. On 11 May 1896, locomotives replaced the cables, much later than on the Lime Street line.

A series of shafts still exists to provide ventilation for the tunnel. These presumably correspond to the shafts dug to excavate the pilot headings. They are in Crown Street, Myrtle Street, Blackburne Place, Rathbone Street and White Street. At Blackburne Place, the depth of the line from the land surface was 92ft. When it opened, visitors were taken down the tunnel for excursions and it must have been quite an impressive day out. Sadly, the tunnel is no longer used and the lower section near the river is blocked with debris and full of water. The tunnel remains more or less intact and could at some future date be reopened, perhaps for tourist use? Consideration has been given to using the Wapping tunnel to provide a rail link from the Central–Hunts Cross Line to the Broadgreen area. Another proposal was to take the M62 into Liverpool using the Wapping and Waterloo tunnels.

Opposite Ventilation shaft for the CLC (Cheshire Lines Commitee) Tunnel at Great George Street.

Above Park Lane end of the Wapping Tunnel with a signal box in the wall.

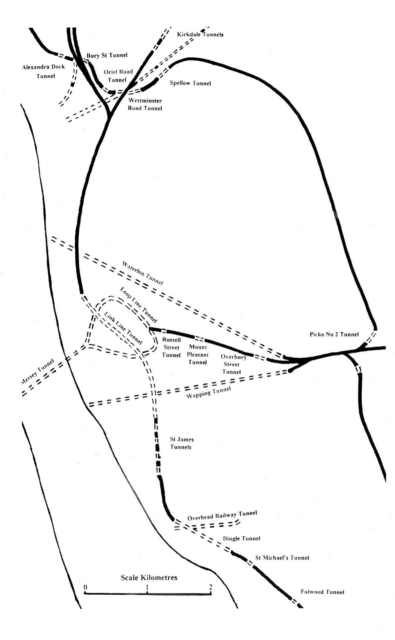

The Waterloo–Victoria Tunnels

The Victoria tunnel is 2706yds long and runs from Edge Hill to where it opens out into an open air section at Byrom Street.

The Waterloo tunnel is 852yds long and is a continuation of the Victoria tunnel. It runs down to the Waterloo Dock and Goods Station. At its lower end, it ran under the Liverpool and Bury Railway (later part of the Lancashire and Yorkshire Railway) which was elevated on viaducts as it ran along parallel to the Mersey shore. In 1849, the Waterloo Goods Station opened and it closed in 1963. In 1873/74, the Waterloo Station was enlarged and, in 1895, the line was extended south to the Riverside Station to meet the passenger liners. The Riverside Station extension was opened on 10 July 1895 and closed in 1971.

The Waterloo–Victoria Tunnel, an arched structure lined with brick, is 26ft wide and can take a double line. The portal at Edge Hill is lined with stone and the portal at the western dockside end is lined with brick. Both lines carried a double railway track and were opened in August 1849.

An 'endless rope' was also used in the Waterloo–Victoria Tunnel; a stationary engine was located at Edge Hill to work it. In February 1895, the rope broke and locomotives took over hauling wagons.

The Northern lines and tunnels

In 1848, the Liverpool and Bury Railway Company constructed a railway line from north of Liverpool into Great Howard Street where a temporary passenger station was built. In 1850, this terminus was extended to Tithebarn Street Station. The delay in the extension of the line to Tithebarn Street was caused by the construction of the Hawkshaw arch. In 1849, the East Lancashire Railway Company also brought the Preston Line into Great Howard Street and Tithebarn Street stations. In 1884-88, Tithebarn Street Station was demolished and Exchange Station was built.

Railways approaching from the north ran over ground that was generally flatter than the ground faced by railways coming from the south. So low was much of this ground that viaducts were built, some of which remain today despite the closure of Exchange Station. The truncated viaduct can be found in the Love Lane area and the arches are still used for lock-ups and workshops. Despite the level ground, several small tunnels were cut in the Kirkdale area.

- Kirkdale Number 1 tunnel is 498yds long and carried the Liverpool, Bolton and Bury Lines under Bedford Road. Kirkdale Number 2 tunnel is 210yds long and carried the Liverpool, Bolton and Bury Lines under Breeze Hill.

- The Bankfield Branch, which ran through St John's Tunnel (109yds long), the Brasenose Road Tunnel (67yds long) and the Canal Tunnel (51yds long) linked the main lines with Bankfield and Canada Dock Goods Station.

- The Cheshire Lines route approaching from Walton had a branch which, after passing through Walton Hill Tunnel (242yds long) under Rice Lane, then Breeze Hill Tunnel (646yds long), ran alongside the Lancashire and Yorkshire and the Liverpool, Bolton and Bury Lines and reached Huskisson Goods and Passenger Stations situated between Bankhall Lane and Boundary Street.

- The Midland Railway had a branch off the Cheshire Lines at Bootle Branch Junction in Fazakerley with the Bootle Branch Tunnel (481yds long) under Marsh Lane before reaching the Alexandra and Langton Goods Stations.

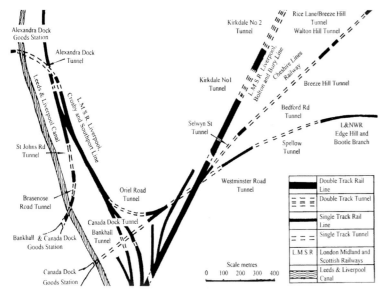

far left The tunnels of North Liverpool
Left The Kirkdale tunnels.

Above left Westminster Road Tunnel with Walton Tunnel on the left.

Above Walton Tunnel.

The Cheshire Lines tunnels

In the 1860s the Manchester, Sheffield and Lincolnshire Railway (MS&L) and the Great Northern Railway (GNR) constructed a railway line into Liverpool and this became the Cheshire Lines Committee (CLC) when the Midland Railway joined them. In 1864, the MS&LR and the GNR built the Garston to Liverpool Line which terminated at Brunswick Station.

In 1880, the CLC built a railway line from Hunts Cross to Huskisson Dock, i.e. an outer loop line. The approach to the city from Garston to the south was along the Mersey shore. Although the land here was reasonably flat, the company constructed several sections of tunnel. The Fulwood Tunnel runs for nearly 200yds under Fulwood Park. A shorter tunnel of 100yds runs under Southwood Road near St Michael's Station. The Dingle Tunnel is much longer and runs for 1082yds from near Buckland Street to where Beresford Road meets Grafton Street.

Passengers travelling into Liverpool along these railway lines at that time had to alight and take a free bus ride into the town centre which was inconvenient. In 1874, the link between Brunswick Dock Station and Central Station was built with an intermediate station, St James Station (closed in 1916) at St James Place on Parliament Street. This extension into Liverpool had to travel underground. It first disappeared under the high ground in Toxteth at Grafton Street. The tunnel ran underground for about 721yds and included:

- St James No 1 – 185yds
- St James No 2 – 172yds
- St James No 3 – 153yds
- St James No 4 – 211yds

Occasionally, gaps in the roof exposed the line to the open air at Upper Mann Street, Beaufort Street, and Hill Street. At St James Place, the station was also open to the air. The Central CLC Tunnel, then continued underground for 1007yds to Central Station at the bottom end of Bold Street. Ventilation shafts were located in Back Berry Street and Great George Street/Raffles Street.

Left The Central CLC Tunnel continued underground for 1007yds to Central Station at the bottom end of Bold Street.

Opposite The CLC line goes under the Overhead Railway Tunnel at the Dingle.

Wavertree Sidings tunnels

The Runcorn Railway Bridge and Line through Allerton and Mossley Hill was built in 1864 to shorten the route to London. It occupied low ground and therefore needed embankments rather than tunnels. Later, when the Edge Hill marshalling yards were built (1873-1881) tunnels, viaducts and bridges were needed so that the traffic to and from the sorting sidings could reach the Edge Hill and Bootle Branch Lines, the Wapping Tunnel, the Victoria/Waterloo Tunnels, the Manchester Line and the main line via Mossley Hill. The tunnels were the Picko Tunnels to the Edge Hill and Bootle Branches under the sidings. They included Picko No 2 (167yds long) and Picko No 1 (52yds long) to Pigue Lane and a second tunnel from Mossley Hill (about 60yds long) under the sidings. The third tunnel was the Olive Mount Tunnel (147yds long) from the Manchester Line to the Bootle Branch.

On the Edge Hill and Bootle Branch line, the first tunnel was the Spellow Tunnel (347yds long) under St Francis de Sales School, Carisbrooke Road, Roxborough Street and Delamore Street. Next came the Westminster Road No 1 (62yds) and the Westminster Road No 2 (276yds) which ran under Westminster Road and the Lancashire and Yorkshire Line to Ormskirk. Here at Atlantic Docks Junction, the Alexandra Dock Branch swung north. Straight on, however, under the Lancashire and Yorkshire Southport Line and the Leeds/Liverpool Canal, was the Canada Dock Tunnel (427yds) leading to the Canada Dock Goods Station. From the Atlantic Docks Junction, the Alexandra Dock Branch swung north through the Oriel Road Tunnel (288yds) under Falstaff, Portia and Romeo Streets. After a connection to the Southport Line, the Berry Street Tunnel (140yds) almost beneath Oriel Road Station took the line quickly to Alexandra Dock Tunnel (117yds) under the Leeds-Liverpool Canal to the Alexandra Goods and Passenger Station.

The Mersey Railway Tunnel

The Mersey Estuary can be said to have made Liverpool as a port but it also made development on the Birkenhead side of the river very difficult. The monks of Birkenhead started a ferry service hundreds of years ago. In 1877, 26 million passenger journeys were made and 750,000 tons of goods were carried on the Mersey ferries. A better crossing would have increased these figures substantially. In 1825, a road tunnel was considered and planned by Isambard Kingdom Brunel of Great Western Railway fame.

The construction of the Birkenhead to Hoylake Railway in 1866, together with the development of steam ferries, made commuting to Liverpool by ferry a viable proposition. It was now possible to live in many parts of North Wirral and work in Liverpool. In 1866, an Act of Parliament was passed which permitted the construction of a railway tunnel under the River Mersey and the project was backed by merchants and industrialists. They proposed a 'pneumatic railway' which would use air pressure to drive the trains. Brunel had used this technology in the south-west of England but with limited success. The pneumatic railway was not a practical proposition given the technology available at that time and a more conventional railway was built.

Construction of the Mersey Railway Tunnel

In 1879, a contract was signed between Major Samuel Isaac and the tunnelling company to sink shafts, erect pumps and drive trial headings towards the river. In December 1879, work had commenced and, in 1880, tunnelling began with vertical shafts sunk at George's Dock in Liverpool and on the Wirral side at Birkenhead. From these shafts, trial headings were driven towards the river. Unfortunately, the contractor constructing the tunnel failed, so Major Isaac took over the operation and completed the project.

Three tunnels were in fact built. The main tunnel was 26ft wide and 19ft high from the rail level to the roof. There was room for two railway tracks side by side. The tunnel was lined with 6-8 layers of brick and

38 million bricks were used for this purpose. The other two tunnels were for drainage and ventilation.

In order to save money, cut and cover methods were planned for excavation in Liverpool itself where the tunnel was near the surface. Unfortunately, the builders encountered strong opposition to this method from traders and residents and had to resort to tunnelling. Despite this, the foundations of several buildings in Hamilton Street were damaged by subsidence.

The work of cutting the tunnel was started using explosives and pick axes. Progress using this method was slow and work progressed at only 10-13yds per week. In February 1883, a new machine, the Beaumont Cutter, driven by compressed air, was introduced and weekly progress was raised considerably. The same machine was used in trial borings for the early Channel Tunnel, which was started around the same time.

The workmen digging the tunnel had the advantage of electric lighting, unlike the men who built the Wapping Tunnel. In January 1884, the two headings met 1,115yds from the Birkenhead shaft and in December 1885, the tunnel was complete and the public were allowed to walk through. On 20 January 1886, the tunnel was opened by the Prince of Wales and, on 1 February, the first public transport was allowed through; 36,000 passengers using the line on the first day.

The construction of the tunnel also allowed a telephone link to be laid between the Liverpool and Birkenhead exchanges, improving the telephone network. Four large 'Guibal' fans were built through a special vent passage 7ft 4ins from the railway to the pumps.

Opposite top Laying cables in the Mersey Railway Tunnel.

Opposite bottom In 1886, a ten foot wide subway was built from James Street Station to Water Street.

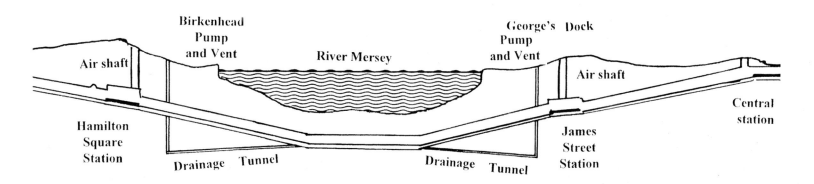

Drainage of the Mersey Railway Tunnel

Drainage was bound to be a major problem under the river and large pumps were built above ground at each of the main shafts on either side of the Mersey. The engines could have been located underground but might have been flooded if the pumps failed. At the base of the main shafts, massive standage headings were excavated which could take 80,000 gallons of water, enough to allow workers to escape should the pumps fail, or a sudden influx of water occur.

Smaller tunnels led from the lowest point on the rail tunnel down to the standage headings, i.e. they sloped towards the land to allow the water to drain away from the tunnel. The pumps could expect to deal with 7,000 to 8,000 gallons of water per minute. The headings for the drainage tunnel were driven at gradients of 1 in 500 and 1 in 900 from the vertical shafts at George's Dock to the Birkenhead shaft up to the central low point of the tunnel. Initially, these tunnels were cut by hand but the Beaumont cutting machines speeded up the work to as much as 65yds per week in the softer rock on the Liverpool side. Ironically, the wettest section of the heading was under the land, rather than the river. The Beaumont machine cut a tunnel 7ft 3ins in diameter but this was widened to 9ft by 8ft to provide enough space for two working roads. The tunnels were lined where the rock was softer but over most of their length this was unnecessary.

The stations

Stations were built at Hamilton Square in Birkenhead and James Street in Liverpool. Both were located 80ft below the surface. They were cut out of rock and were 400ft long, 50ft wide and 30ft high. Gas lights were used in the stations and tunnel itself as gas was more reliable than electricity at this time and a gas works was built at Birkenhead to provide the gas. The locomotives travelling along the tunnel were special six wheel tank engines.

The stations were also provided with lifts. The lift cages were 20ft long by 17ft wide and 8ft 10ins high. They could take 100 people at any one time and were worked hydraulically from a 120ft high tower over Hamilton Square Station. A similar water tower at James Street was damaged during the war and had to be demolished but the Hamilton Square Station water tower still exists. In 1886, a 10ft wide subway was built from James Street Station to Water Street.

Underground extensions and links

In January 1888, a branch line was opened from Hamilton Square to Birkenhead Park. In 1891, the Birkenhead line was extended from Green Lane to Rock Ferry and, in March 1895, a connection to the Birkenhead-Chester line was built.

On 11 January 1892, the line on the Liverpool side of the river was extended from James Street to Central Station (low level). Its alignment was adjusted to link up with the line from St James Tunnel. The construction of the Bold Street link ran under Lord Street and Church Street and hit severe problems. Because the station and its approaches were very near the surface, the roof had to be supported with iron girders. The entire roadway at Ranelagh Place had to be removed and replaced with heavy timbers until the tunnel was finished and now Ranelagh Place rests on girders supported by brick and cement supports. To avoid traffic problems, much of the roadway work was done at night. The section of line under the Central Station Booking Hall was taken through three separate tunnels to spread the weight. The tunnels were only 14ft below the booking station and its walls had to be underpinned.

Subways and stairs were constructed to give access to the station from Waterloo Place and the basement of the Lyceum was used as a waiting room. A hydraulic lift was installed for luggage. At its widest, the underground station was 55ft wide and a row of steel columns on the platform carried girders which supported Central Station. Excavated rock was carried to trucks stationed on the railway lines below and then railed to the Wirral for use as track ballast. As explosives could not be used, all the rock was excavated by hand. Soft clay layers in the sandstone had to be excavated and refilled with brick to stop sliding. Guibal fans were installed to ventilate this station and, together with a large chimney, were located at the eastern end of Central Station.

The lower tunnel extension did not link up with the Cheshire Lines until the Link Line was constructed in the 1970s. The total length of the tunnel from Hamilton Square to Central Station is 1 mile 1,430yds.

Electrification of the Mersey Railway Tunnel

In 1890, the Mersey Railway Tunnel carried 10 million passengers. Unfortunately, there was a severe smoke problem as the ventilation system was inadequate. As a result, the decision was taken in 1899 to electrify the Mersey Tunnel line and, by 1903, the electrification was complete; the first such electrification in the world. This was followed, in 1938, by the electrification of the West Kirby and New Brighton Line and a through rail route to North Wirral was now possible without changing trains.

In 1886, a tunnel was planned from the Cheshire lines Central Railway Station to Huskisson Dock but this was never built.

The New Link Line

In 1962, as part of the integration of Merseyside transport, the Railway Link Line was proposed to link up the Southport and Ormskirk lines with the other railways approaching Liverpool from the east and south. In 1967-68 Liverpool City Corporation sponsored a Parliamentary Bill to carry out the rail improvements and, in 1968, the Mersey Railway Extension Act was passed, under which the Merseyside Passenger Transport Executive, the MPTE, was formed. The Link Line was built by the British Railways Board and the electrification was extended to Garston and Kirkby. Seventy-five per cent of the construction costs were met by the Ministry of Transport. In 1974, Merseyside County was formed and the County Council endorsed the proposed co-ordination and integration of transport.

The Link Line started just south of the Hawkshaw Arch and rapidly descended to pass under Leeds Street where the first sections were built using the 'cut and cover' technique. From there, twin bore tunnels were cut to a point just past the site of the original Cavern Club where they joined up to the double track single bore original Mersey Railway Tunnel at Paradise Street Junction. Working shafts had been constructed at Moorfields and the Cavern Site.) Beyond Central Station, the floor of the disused CLC Tunnel was lowered to join up with the Central Low Level Station of the Mersey Railway. However, it was envisaged that a branch would be built to connect with the Broadgreen line via the Wapping tunnel so that an additional single bore tunnel was also constructed parallel to the CLC Tunnel to enable a 'flying' or 'burying' junction to be constructed at a later date to avoid conflicting train movements. Short headings were also made to avoid disruptions to train services, should this line ever be built.

Reverting back to Paradise Street Junction, a single line connection has been left in between the Link and the Loop Lines along the Old Mersey Railway Tunnel, to enable stock transfers to be made, but this is never used for passenger services. One new station was built on the Link Line at Moorfields which allowed Exchange Station to close, while the old Central Low Level Station was refurbished to serve Southport instead of the Wirral.

The New Loop Line

The line consists of a single line loop, 3·2 kilometres long, 4·6 metres in diameter with traffic moving only in a clockwise direction. There are five stations along the line: Moorfields deep level, Lime Street deep level, Central Station and two James Street Stations.

During 1972-73, headings were cut in sandstone from four vertical shafts at Mann Island, Moorfields, William Brown Street and Central Station. The depth of the tunnel varied from 17·6 metres to 37·8 metres. The nearness of the Loop Line to the surface is obvious to anyone who has visited theatres and shop basements in Liverpool. Unlike the Old River Tunnel, the Loop Line was lined with concrete. The excavating machine, developed by Dosco Engineering, had a rotating head with hardened steel teeth located on a

Left The New Loop Line, construction of the new tunnel at Moorfields.

Below left The excavating machine, developed by Dosco Engineering, had a rotating head with hardened steel teeth located on a swinging boom. Three of these excavators were used to cut away the rock. The maximum cutting speed reached 57 metres of tunnel in one week and lasers were used to keep the tunnel on line.

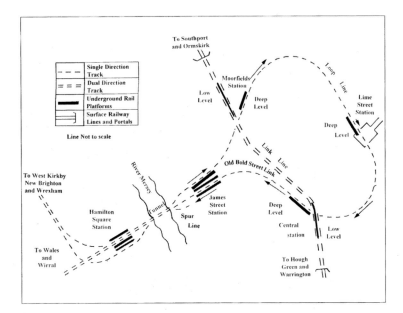

swinging boom. Three of these excavators were used to cut away the rock. The maximum cutting speed reached 57 metres of tunnel in one week and lasers were used to keep the tunnel on line.

The lines beyond Hamilton Square Station needed remodelling as the Rock Ferry and Birkenhead Park lines cross at this point and traffic control was needed. This needed modification in the light of the great volumes of traffic which the new line was expected to generate. The Birkenhead Park line was taken beneath the Rock Ferry line and a new platform built at Hamilton Square Station. These changes would have allowed the trains between Birkenhead and Liverpool to run every two minutes but, in practice, one every five minutes has sufficed.

Running the Loop Line is not an easy matter. The biggest problem is water; like all the other tunnels, the Loop Line tends to leak. Pumps were erected at both ends of the Mersey Railway Tunnel at George's Dock and Birkenhead and also at Central Station. Weep holes in the Loop Line Tunnel allow the water to flow into the tunnel and this water drains down a channel in the tunnel floor to a sump and pump at Central Station. The water is pumped out and sold to the Liverpool Daily Post and Echo and they sell hot water on to the Royal Insurance. Of the 1000 gallons per minute which flow into the Loop Line, 300 gallons per minute are pumped out at Central Station and the other 700 gallons per minute drain down to George's Dock and are pumped out there. This solves the flooding problem but corrosion rates are much higher in a wet tunnel and repair costs on the Loop Line are extremely high. Railway lines need to be replaced every two years compared to every 15-20 years above ground. The rate of inflow varies along the length of the Loop Line and is greatest at Lime Street where the line crosses a fault. The water is salty and particularly 'aggressive' causing corrosion of concrete and electricity leakage. The water table can never be allowed to reach its former level as the tunnels will flood. Some existing boreholes which are not being used for commercial or domestic abstraction are still used to monitor ground water levels, specifically at Edge Hill and 'Reece's Restaurant' in the city centre.

The Overhead Railway

The Overhead Railway may seem to be a very odd topic to include in this book but its construction involved considerable tunnelling. The 'Dockers' Umbrella', as it came to be known, was built in the 1890s and opened on 6 March 1893. At first, the railway terminated at Alexandra Dock and an extension, opened a year later, took the line north to Seaforth. The southern extension from Herculaneum to the Dingle was opened on 21 December 1896. The Overhead Railway line ran all the way from Seaforth in the north, to Dingle in the south, a distance of 7 miles 160yds. Most of this route ran along an elevated track carried on iron girders. The remains of the vertical supports can still be seen in the walls along the dock road.

The Overhead Railway Tunnel

At the southern end of the line, the Overhead Railway swung inland over the ground-level railways and along a viaduct and bridge. Just to the north of Herculaneum Dock, it went straight into the side of the sandstone hill at Grafton Street in the Dingle and is clearly visible today. As the line went straight into the side of the hill, it crossed over the Dingle Railway Tunnel on the Cheshire Lines Railway. At least 2ft 9ins of rock separated the two tunnels vertically and additional support was provided in the form of a segmental screen arch over the Cheshire Lines Tunnel. A condition of the construction was that the Overhead Railway Tunnel was to allow for a second Cheshire Lines Tunnel to the east of the existing tunnel but this was never built.

The Overhead Railway Tunnel is just under half a mile long and terminates at Dingle Railway Station on Park Road. The first 605yds of the tunnel was 25ft 6ins wide and 19ft high. As the line approached the station, the tunnel widened to 52ft with a height of 24ft 6ins for a distance of 163yds. The final 41yds had the same dimensions as the first 605yds and the tunnel ended with a vertical wall of rock. The wider section of the tunnel housed the underground station, which at the time was the largest tunnel arch in Britain. In the centre of the station, was an island platform 170ft long and 28ft wide. Stairs at the eastern end of the station took the passengers up to the surface and the booking hall on Park Road. The station and tunnel were illuminated by electric lights.

The construction of the Overhead Railway Tunnel

Five shafts 10ft square were sunk along the line of the tunnel and from these shafts headings were cut in both directions. These headings met with remarkable accuracy, unlike the Wapping Tunnel many years earlier. Black powder explosives, along with pick axes, were used in the digging of the tunnel. Where the Overhead Railway Tunnel crossed over the Cheshire Lines Tunnel, explosives were not used and here the work was all done by hand – an expensive undertaking. A sewer above the line of the tunnel route also needed support and modifications to the tunnel arch had to be made to prevent damage to the sewer. Although the tunnel was cut into sandstone, it was not always easy to excavate. Wet clay layers made the working conditions difficult and stout timbering was needed to shore up the rock. A lining of brindle brick was essential throughout.

During the war, bombing caused extensive damage to the Overhead Railway but was quickly repaired. In February 1956, fire gutted a station building at Seaforth and damage costing £30,00 was caused to two trains. Arson was suspected when a tyre was found in one of the trains.

After the war, the Overhead Railway needed modernisation and, although some work was done, the cost of repairs, estimated at two million pounds, was beyond the resources of the company and the line closed on 30 December 1956.

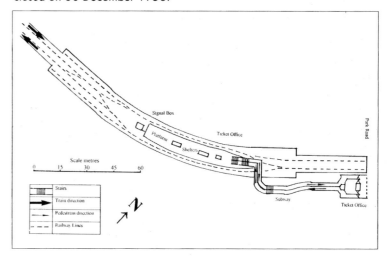

The stations

Liverpool has four underground stations:

- James Street Station is the oldest of the underground stations and has a tunnel providing pedestrian access to Water Street.

- Moorfields Station with separate platforms on the Loop and Link Lines has a tunnel connecting it to the business district around Old Hall Street. It also has a commemorative plaque to Vivien Hughes (1909-1994), a civil engineer who played a major part in the development of Liverpool's Underground Railway system and who was born and died within sight and sound of the railway.

- Lime Street Station, the surface part of which goes back to 1836. The underground station was built at the same time as the Loop Line. Much of the station and booking area is under St George's Plateau which provides a convenient second pedestrian underground crossing to Lime Street. Like all the other stations there are stairs and escalators as well as a lift for those who need it.

- Central Station is interesting because it has two clear levels. The main pedestrian exits are to Ranelagh and Bold Street but there are others to Fairclough Street and Lewis's department store.

Conclusion

Since the war, many of Liverpool's railway lines have closed. However, many of the tunnels remain and who knows what may happen in the future? Perhaps an individual or organisation will come along with the initiative and imagination and resources, to make constructive use of them.

THE MERSEY TUNNEL — June 18th 1929.

A.1. (Contract No 2.) Looking from Liverpool on Line of Tunnel.

Roads under the Mersey

Early days

Liverpool has long suffered from the fact that it lies on a wide estuary which is difficult to cross. The monks of Birkenhead started a ferry which provided the main link between Birkenhead and Liverpool for hundreds of years. Warrington was for many years the lowest bridging point on the Mersey and improvements in cross-river communications were badly needed. During the last century, the 'Transporter', a massive platform slung from a gigantic metal overhead frame, was built at the Runcorn/Widnes crossing. This platform had to fill and empty like a ferry and those old enough may remember the chronic delays to traffic seeking to cross at that point. Something had to be done!

The first tunnel crossing was proposed in 1825 and, again, in 1827. A report in 1830 rejected the road tunnel because it could have presented a danger to buildings. Liverpool City Council also considered that any tunnel would be of more advantage to Birkenhead than to Liverpool. The Mersey Railway Tunnel was completed in 1886 and this effectively reduced the need for a road tunnel and delayed the project. The rail tunnel provided easier access for commuters from the Wirral but commerce and industry still had a problem and a link was needed for lorries.

A suspension bridge was proposed which would have loomed high over the Mersey and would have cost £10,550,000, a staggering sum at that time. During the nineteenth century, the Mersey Estuary was a hive of activity with ferries and thousands of ships plying the river each year. The danger from fog and gales which could have caused accidents and delays made the bridge a less popular option. Vulnerability in time of war and high maintenance costs were also considered although a bridge would have provided a spectacular attraction for Merseyside.

Queensway

A road tunnel was a cheaper option and, in 1922, a co-ordinating committee was set up under Sir Archibald Salvidge, Chairman of Liverpool City Council. The co-ordinating committee had representatives from the towns of Birkenhead, Wallasey, Liverpool and Bootle, as the final location of the tunnel had not yet been decided. The committee proposed a 44ft wide circular tunnel with two entrances. The planned tunnel was large enough for four 9ft carriageways, which could run along the top half of the tunnel and two tramlines could run along the

bottom. At first, only two entrances were proposed and the cost of construction was estimated at over £6,400,000. Not everyone was pleased with the proposal and the railway and ferry companies saw the tunnel as a threat to their own livelihoods. They felt that the road tunnel would carry fewer passengers than the existing crossings and charge higher fares. The Mersey Docks and Harbour Company were also very concerned that a road tunnel would restrict dock development in Cheshire. Wallasey and Bootle dropped out of the scheme leaving Birkenhead and Liverpool to complete the plans.

On 8 August 1925, the necessary Act of Parliament was passed and the Royal Assent given for the new Mersey Road Tunnel. It was to be called 'Queensway' in honour of Queen Mary, the wife of King George V. Sir Basil Mott, an experienced tunnel engineer who had worked on London underground tunnels, was the main architect. John Brodie, Liverpool's City Engineer, and Sir Maurice Fitzmaurice were also members of the planning team.

Finance was a different problem. In September 1924, the government offered £2,375,000 towards the cost of the tunnel, on condition that it was toll free. The remaining finance would have imposed a heavy burden on the ratepayers with no way of raising money from tolls. However, a new government, headed by Stanley Baldwin was elected in November 1924, and in January 1925, Winston Churchill in the Treasury offered £2,500,000 and allowed tolls for the first 20 years of operation. More parliamentary bills followed in 1927 and 1928.

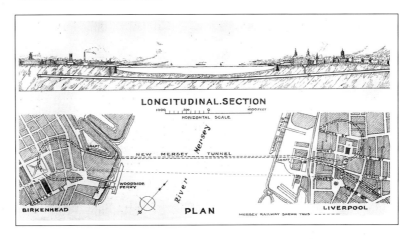

LONGITUDINAL.SECTION

Right In December 1925, construction work began with two hundred foot vertical rock shafts being sunk at the dry disused George's Dock and at Birkenhead.

Opposite The planned tunnel was large enough for four carriageways measuring nine feet wide, which could run along the top half of the tunnel and two tramlines to run along the bottom.

Construction

In December 1925, construction work began with 200ft vertical rock shafts being sunk at the dry disused George's Dock and at Birkenhead. The Princess Royal, Princess Mary turned a golden key to start the pneumatic drills at George's Dock in Liverpool, whilst Sir Archibald Salvidge wielded the first pick in Birkenhead. Two smaller pilot tunnels were cut along the proposed line, one above the other. Each pilot tunnel was 12ft high and 15ft wide, similar in size to the London Underground tunnels, many of which had been cut over the previous half century.

In Liverpool, there had been some debate over the location of the tunnel entrance and the final decision was the Old Haymarket, behind St George's Hall, as the site required minimal demolition. The Birkenhead entrance was built in Chester Street, on the site of the Carnegie Library, which had to be demolished. Two extra entrances were added to serve both the Liverpool and Birkenhead docks. The pilot tunnels met and Sir Archibald Salvidge cut through the rock divide with a pick axe. The alignment of the two headings was only one inch out. On 3 April 1928, the Lord Mayor of Liverpool, Margaret Bevan, shook hands with the Mayor of Birkenhead, Alderman Frederick Taylor, through the hole in the rock divide. In fact, the breakthrough occurred one week before and the hole was repaired to await the ceremony and handshake.

The real work of digging the main tunnel then started with the engineers hoping to avoid some of the problems which had affected the railway tunnel. The first stage was to excavate the top half of the tunnel and the rubble was driven away at night in lorries. As the tunnel progressed, the walls were lined with bolted, flanged, cast-iron plates and backfilled with rubble which was then grouted. A trial enlarging of the two pilot headings was made over a 300ft length between the Birkenhead shaft and the Woodside shore to check for problems. The central river section of the tunnel was circular with a diameter of 44ft and it was lined top and bottom with cast-iron plates. At the two ends, the bottom half of the tunnel was only partially-excavated. The bottom half of the tunnel was lined with bolted, flanged, cast-iron plates and the top half with curved steel joists set in concrete.

The two pilot tunnels proved very useful, as the tunnellers were able to cut chutes from the upper to the lower heading. The rock excavated from the top tunnel was dropped down onto an electric railway and removed. Later, a suspended roadway was built to allow work on the

upper half to continue unhindered, while the lower half was being excavated. Teams of men called 'break-ups' worked on different sections of the tunnel simultaneously, in order to speed up construction. At the two entrances, a 'cut and fill' technique was used where the roof was thinner but this was not possible under Dale Street where a special roof shield had to be used. This worked well except at the junction of Hatton Garden and Dale Street. Here a roof collapse occurred killing two tunnellers, due to the presence of unforeseen excavations dating back to Cromwell's siege of Liverpool Castle.

After all joints were sealed with lead, the lined tunnel was cleaned and a gunite rendering of cement, consisting of sand and a waterproofing agent was sprayed under pressure onto the walls. The gunite was in turn coated with a bituminous emulsion and, after a coating of plaster, a final layer of paint was applied. These coatings were applied from timber gantries mounted on wheels.

In the cross section on the previous page we can see the roadway, which was made of reinforced concrete, spanned the tunnel 18ins below the centre line and was carried on two reinforced concrete walls 18ft apart. Nearer the entrances, the road was carried on two sets of concrete pillars 7ft apart. The original road was made of cast-iron plates set in bitumen and this was replaced with bitumen and hard mastic. A paved walkway ran along each side, the full length of the tunnel. Black glass lined both sides but was later replaced by white vitrolite and later again by PVC-coated steel. The entrances were lined with Portland Limestone and stone pylons stood beside each portal. Four double-sided booths were built at each end of the tunnel to collect tolls and emergency exits were built at the two vertical dock shafts.

Problems

It was anticipated that water would be one of the main problems as the rock through which the tunnel was cut was permeable Bunter Sandstone and numerous fractures and fissures allowed water to flow into the tunnel. On the Liverpool side, where the rocks were more permeable, 24,000 gallons of water per minute flowed into the tunnel. As the headings moved down the line of the tunnel, 40ft holes were drilled up into the rock and grout was injected into these holes under great pressure in order to slow the flow of water. Drainage tunnels were cut from the bottom of both the George's Dock and the Birkenhead shafts upwards at a gradient of 1 in 500 to the centre of the river where the

tunnel reached its lowest point. Water then drained down to both shafts and was pumped out. After the two heading tunnels met in the centre of the river, all the water drained down to the Liverpool shaft. The cast-iron casing effectively sealed the tunnel. There was some seepage of water but this proved manageable and, in fact, remarkably little water seeps into the tunnel today. Where this happens, it may be due to the presence of a fault and it is possible that more water is carried in by vehicles entering the tunnel in wet weather than flows in from leaks.

A small spur tunnel exists off the main tunnel on the Liverpool side which was cut to house the ponies which hauled the trucks of rock around. This section of tunnel is unlined and so leaks a little more. Gas also used to accumulate in the tunnel and constant testing was necessary.

Digging the tunnel was a hazardous occupation and the work was hard and wet. Seventeen hundred men were employed on the construction and salt boils were common. No workman was allowed to work by himself but this did not stop casualties and, in all, there were nineteen fatalities. When one of the workmen, Bert Jones, was killed by a falling rock, his workmates took the day off without pay to attend his funeral.

Twelve million tons of rock were excavated and much of it went for the construction of the new promenade at Otterspool. On the Birkenhead side, the rock was used to fill in Storeton Quarry (where many dinosaur footprints had been found before quarrying operations finished).

Ventilation was a further concern since cars presented a very different set of problems from those created by the railways. Tests on the Holland Tunnel in America revealed that the planned ventilation system would prove inadequate and massive new 28ft fan vents were designed by Herbert Rowse. The extra £2 million cost incurred by the revised ventilation plans must have given the sponsors a shock. This raised the final construction cost to £7,723,000. A fourth Bill was passed by Parliament and the imposition of tolls was permitted for the first 40 years of operation. Six ventilation shafts were constructed which could remove 2,500,000 cubic feet of air per minute. The fresh air was drawn in at the vent and down into the lower part of the tunnel. It rose in the central lower section of the tunnel below the walkway and the exhaust travelled up the roadway to the entrance.

Herbert Rowse, who had designed the new Philharmonic Hall, also designed the ventilation buildings and their decor, the toll booths and

THE MERSEY TUNNEL

Right Excavating the lower part of the tunnel with a temporary suspended roadway in the roof section.

Opposite The nearly complete tunnel lined with bolted cast iron plates.

THE MERSEY TUNNEL
DURING CONSTRUCTION
STEWART BALE
COMMERCIAL PHOTOGRAPHER
LIVERPOOL

Right Despite the use of machinery, a lot of hand digging took place.

Opposite Painting the arch of the tunnel white improved illumination.

lighting. His work is now highly regarded and the tunnel vents and portals are Department of the Environment listed structures.

The tram lanes which were intended to run below the main roadway were never constructed and the lower 'deck' was simply used for utilities such as power cables.

The Grand Opening

The new tunnel was opened to the public on 17 December 1933. At Easter 1934, 80,000 members of the public were allowed to walk through the tunnel for a charge of sixpence, the proceeds going to charity. On 18 July 1934, the tunnel was officially opened by King George V and Queen Mary, who had also opened Walton Hall Park earlier in the day. It was a great celebration with many local and government dignitaries present and a parade of troops. Two massive curtains were meant to be raised to reveal the new tunnel, but the opening mechanism failed and the curtains had to be cranked open by hand. A cortege of cars carrying the royal guests and dignitaries drove through the tunnel to Birkenhead where King George opened the new Borough Road Library, built to replace the Carnegie Library demolished to allow the construction of the tunnel entrance. Statues of King George V and Queen Mary stood behind the portal in the Old Haymarket but have since been moved to a position on either side of the portal.

The tunnel proved very popular and even became a tourist attraction. Horse-drawn vehicles had to continue to use the ferry although the original plans had envisaged slower animal traffic using the tunnel. Indeed, concern over the future of the ferries was such that public bus services were banned from the tunnel until the 1970s. Unfortunately, the use of the ferries did decline and it is difficult to see how this could have been prevented. Ferry services are now a shadow of their former glory. Today, the public is in too much of a hurry for the leisurely ferry crossing. The tunnel, by contrast, thrived.

Traffic levels rose as more and more people bought cars and the general public had more time and money for leisure. Commuter use of the tunnel rose despite the tolls. By 1953, eight million vehicles were using the tunnel each year and severe traffic problems were developing. The traffic lights installed to control the traffic from the dock entrances caused further delays and their use was discontinued. The Birkenhead Dock entrance has now closed and the Liverpool Dock entrance is only used for traffic leaving the tunnel. Some relief was

provided by the construction of the Runcorn/Widnes bridge in 1961. By 1968, traffic levels had increased to 19 million vehicles per year and something had to be done. Roads were reorganised with flyovers and queuing lights, but these could not solve the problem of excessive traffic and the inevitable, rush-hour delays.

An additional crossing was the only answer and the old tunnel versus. bridge debate resurfaced. In 1958, a joint committee was once again set up to look at the problem. Despite the decline in ferry traffic and shipping, a second tunnel was proposed.

The Kingsway Tunnel

The second tunnel was called Kingsway, despite having a queen on the British throne at the time. Liverpool, Birkenhead and Wallasey agreed to sponsor a new tunnel which would connect to the M53 motorway and, in doing so, they would be able to use the old railway cutting of the former Liverpool and North-West railway as an approach road on the Wallasey side.

The Royal Assent was given for the new tunnel in 1965 and it was decided that it would be simpler to construct two tunnels. Each of these tunnels would be 24ft wide and could take two 12ft wide lanes, much wider than the 9ft lanes in the Queensway Tunnel. In January 1966, a twelve-foot arched pilot tunnel was cut by a small 'mole'. These moles were much faster and more accurate than the machines used in the construction of the Queensway Tunnel and the pilot tunnel took only twelve months to cut.

Construction of the Kingsway Tunnel

The main tunnels were cut separately by a larger 350 ton mole that had been built for the construction of the Mangla Dam diversion tunnels in India and adapted for use in this tunnel. The rotating head of the mole had a 33ft 11ins cutting disc with 55 cutters. It was the first time such a machine was used on a British tunnelling project and, at the time, it was the largest in the world. The ground-up stone was removed on a conveyer belt. Construction of the main tunnel began in the summer of 1967 and, under favourable conditions, the mole was able to cut up to 4ft an hour, although a more realistic figure was 200ft per week.

There was no glacial clay above this tunnel and the roof collapsed regularly with water turning the working area into a mire and slowing progress. Holes were drilled in the roof and grout was injected to seal

THE MERSEY TUNNEL
SYSTEM OF VENTILATION

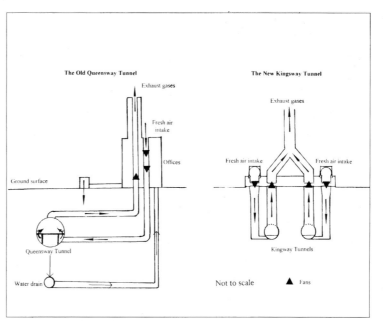

The Old Queensway Tunnel

Exhaust gases

Fresh air intake

Ground surface

Offices

Queensway Tunnel

Water drain

The New Kingsway Tunnel

Exhaust gases

Fresh air intake   Fresh air intake

Kingway Tunnels

Not to scale   ▲ Fans

the rock and fissures but, as in the 1930s, this was only partially successful. As the tunnel progressed, it was lined with concrete sections which were cast and stored in a disused quarry near Mold.

One particularly weak spot was a fault in the centre of the river, which had been identified in the pilot tunnel and the fault zone had been braced and grouted. This was not very effective however and, when the mole approached, a 16ft cavity opened in the roof presenting a very real hazard. Wooden shuttering was erected and concrete was sprayed into the cavity behind it, creating an 80ft umbrella. Despite the success of this measure, work was halted for six weeks at the end of 1968.

At 4pm on 20 February 1968, the main bearing fractured, causing another six-week delay and leading to a storage problem for the concrete lining sections. The bearing had to be replaced in the tunnel because the mole could not be removed as the rings of concrete installed behind the mole had reduced the diameter of the tunnel preventing it from moving backwards.

At the Liverpool end of the tunnel, the mole emerged into clay 500ft from the Liverpool Portal. Pneumatic tools were used on the clay and the tunnel was lined with sections of cast iron. A special shaft was sunk and the mole withdrawn and a massive, arched cover was built over the Liverpool Portal.

The cutting of the second tunnel needed no pilot tunnel and went much more smoothly, with the breakthrough occurring on 4 March 1970.

The ventilation, electrical works and the road itself, took another year to complete. As with the first tunnel, the public was allowed to walk through for a small fee which went to charity. The Queen opened the tunnel on the 24 June 1971 and was then driven through to Wallasey, where a plaque was unveiled. One third of the cross-river vehicular traffic was soon using the tunnel and this rapidly rose to half. This took the pressure off the Queensway Tunnel and, by 1975, the traffic using Queensway soon declined to 1959 levels. By 1982, the predicted traffic levels of 49 million vehicles had not been realised; in fact, it was only 25 million vehicles per year. The traffic using the tunnel has risen slowly and fitfully depending on the state of the local, regional and national economy.

The Mersey tunnels today

The Joint Committee was replaced with the formation of Merseyside Country Council in 1974 which was, in turn, abolished and replaced by the Mersey Passenger Transport Authority in 1984. Buses were permitted to use the tunnel in 1972 and by 1986, bus services had been deregulated.

Being straighter, with wider lanes and separate traffic flows, speeds of 40mph are permitted compared with 30mph in the old tunnel. Many drivers on the M53 are reluctant to slow to the 40mph limit on the approach cutting through Wallasey but speed cameras exercise a check on the more exuberant drivers. How many drivers have found themselves on their way to Liverpool having missed the Wallasey turn off? The tight curves at the Liverpool exit have necessitated a similar speed limit, with traffic slowing to 30mph and speeding is more difficult.

Access was speeded up with the installation of automatic booths. Drivers with the correct money throw the toll fee into a basket from where it is conveyed underground, automatically counted and bagged. A few manned booths are available to give change and for lorries. A new Automatic Revenue Collection scheme (ARC) was introduced in 1983 for regular users such as fleet vehicles. These users have a device fitted to their car which automatically registers as it passes through and the user is then billed.

Having two tunnels allows some flexibility. In the morning, the Wirral traffic takes over three lanes and, in the evening, three lanes are available for cars returning to the Wirral.

Accidents are rare because the general public exercises more care in the tunnel situation but, nevertheless, some people still insist on changing lanes. Such people are identified from surveillance cameras and prosecuted and, because breakdowns create long queues, substantial surcharges are imposed on drivers who break down through negligence, such as running out of petrol.

Hazardous cargoes are strictly monitored by the tunnel police and some are banned completely whilst others are allowed through under strictly-controlled circumstances, such as with a police escort or only in specific quantities.

The tunnels are still in debt which currently runs into many millions of pounds but will eventually be eliminated. At the present time, the revenue raised from tolls pays for:

- running costs and personnel
- upkeep and maintenance
- debt servicing (interest)
- some capital repayment

At the time of writing, the toll for a saloon car is £1·00, the same price as in 1992. When the tunnel first opened the toll was one shilling which, at today's prices, would be £1·74, so motorists are getting a good deal.

Conclusion

With the construction of the M56 motorway, the Runcorn/Widnes Bridge has probably provided the competition which has prevented the traffic from reaching anticipated levels. The construction of the M57 extension, the A5300 to the 'Ford Road' may provide more competition for the tunnels.

The 1980s saw the plans put forward for a Mersey Barrage but there are very strong environmental objections to the scheme and it may never be built. The planned barrage would have carried a road, but whether it would have been open to the public is uncertain.

There is, however, talk of a third tunnel south of Hale Point which would also compete with the existing tunnels. The general public may complain about the tunnels and their cost but, perhaps, they should see them as an asset and a feature which results from the unique geography of Merseyside.

Joseph Williamson – The King of Edge Hill

To many Liverpudlians, Joseph Williamson is regarded as one of the most noteworthy and interesting local characters. His nicknames include 'the Mole of Edge Hill', the 'Mad Mole' and the 'the King of Edge Hill'. Eccentric he certainly was; mad he almost certainly was not! Some observers credit him with pioneering the first job-creation schemes. Admittedly, some of the jobs he created were pointless – he is reported to have paid men to dig holes and fill them in again, whilst at other times he would have them moving rocks around from one place to another and then moving them back again. However, most of the time his workers spent their time digging tunnels and building houses.

Joseph Williamson was born in Warrington on 10 March 1769. His father was 'the greatest rip that ever walked on two feet' and his mother was 'a decent woman' who took care of Joseph as best she could. At the age of eleven, he came to Liverpool to work for a tobacco manufacturer, Thomas Tate. Tate's tobacco factory was in Parr Street and his office was in Wolstenholme Square. He may well have lived with the Tates as he states that his mother would not have let Joseph come to Liverpool unless he could lodge with his employer. Joseph Williamson must have impressed Thomas Tate and his daughter Elizabeth as he and Betty were married on 12 December 1802 at St Thomas's Church at the lower end of Park Road.

It was at this point that signs of his eccentricity first appeared. On the day of his wedding, after the ceremony, he went hunting with the Liverpool Hunt and sent his wife home! Today, this treatment of his wife would be considered the equivalent of going to Anfield or Goodison following a midday wedding. Stonehouse suggests that Williamson may have gone on to the hunt in his wedding clothes, which caused quite a stir: 'I went to the hunt as I was, and my uncommonly gay appearance excited the attention of my friends'. In 1803, his father-in-law died and the tobacco business was run by Joseph after his marriage to Betty.

On one occasion, whilst regretting the loss of his bachelor status, he opened the door of his wife's aviary and released all her birds, declaring that it was a pity that married men did not have wings so they could enjoy their liberty again. At other times, he showed a more caring side, for example, when he built her a rockery on the terrace after she had seen a similar one when visiting her friend in Crosby. When she died in 1822, he missed her and declared that he was 'sorry to part with the old girl when she did go'. The two led a 'cat and dog' life of it and it can be presumed that he was not an easy man to live with and she must have been a tolerant and patient wife.

Opposite The double arch entrance on the east side of the corporation stables yard.

Left The painting of Joseph Williamson in Edge Hill Library.

In 1806, Joseph Williamson purchased a property called the 'Long Broom Field' in Edge Hill which was then on the outskirts of town. It was next to the property purchased by Mr Mason in 1800 and after whom Mason Street was named. Williamson's property was bound by Mason Street to the east, Smithdown Lane to the west, Grinfield Street to the south and the Mason's property to the north.

Williamson had a house built on the west side of Mason Street on a terrace which formed the higher part of his property. This probably commanded a good view over Liverpool which lay about one mile to the west. However, since he spent most of his time living below ground, the view would have made little difference. His house was almost as unusual as his excavations, having few windows and a main living room which was described by Stonehouse as an excavated cellar with a vaulted roof and a single window at one end. The window tax certainly concerned him, as in many other properties, he made sure that the windows he installed incurred the minimum tax. It is even suggested that his rockery may have been built to conceal his windows. We are told that his bedroom was more like a den for a wild beast than the dwelling place of a human-being. At one end of the room was a hollowed-out area where he kept his casks of port and sherry.

Stonehouse describes Joseph Williamson as a hospitable man, handing out tumblers of wine to visitors and ale or porter to his workmen. There are well-documented accounts of these visitors, one of whom was Robert Stephenson whose railway tunnel crossed the line of Williamson's tunnels. At other times, he appeared brusque and discouraged visitors. Richard Whittington-Egan describes the most famous example of Williamson's peculiar hospitality – his celebrated 'beanfeast'. On this occasion, he invited a number of guests for dinner and offered them a simple meal of bacon and beans in a none too sumptuous setting, upon which some of his visitors became disgusted and left. At this point, he declared 'Now that I know who really are my friends, pray follow me upstairs', and led them up to a much more lavish feast.

Although he was rich, he did not vaunt his wealth in the usual ways. In the manner of many eccentrics, he cared little for clothes and was always to be seen in a black beaver top hat which Stonehouse describes as a 'shocking bad one'. He wore a patched brown coat and corduroy breeches and according to Stonehouse his shoes were black and slovenly. His manner varied from rough and uncouth to kind and considerate. Although he liked children, we are not told of any

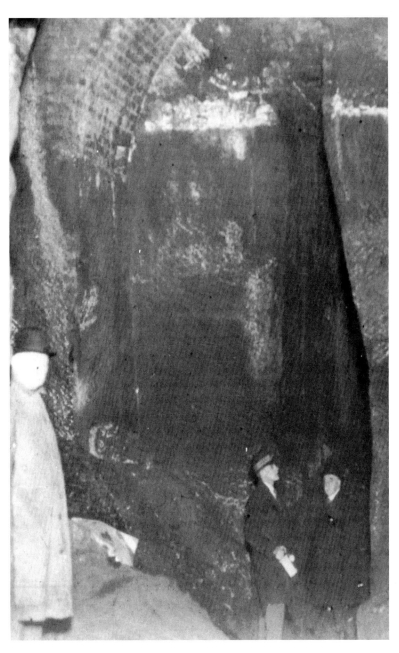

Williamson offspring. George IV met him and described him as 'the only gentleman I met in Liverpool'.

Williamson was a church-goer, as were many people at that time and more than one clergyman was lodged in his houses. He even declared that had he gone into the church he might have become a bishop.

One of his other sources of income was property, the construction and repair of these dwellings being supervised by himself. His qualities as a landlord were as variable as his friendliness. When approached one day by an attractive lady who needed rented accommodation at a reasonable price, he was at first brusque and dismissive. Nevertheless, he went on to find the lady a house and, when it was not quite suitable, he altered the house immediately to suit her wishes. How many landlords today would go out of their way to such an extent? In fact, Stonehouse tells us that Williamson took a great fancy to her and called her the 'Queen of Edge Hill'. When she needed more space, he immediately extended the house by adding a large room which turned out to be one of his own rooms.

Joseph Williamson died on the first of May 1840 and was buried in St Thomas's Churchyard in Park Road, in the Tate family vault. When St Thomas's Church was demolished in 1905, the churchyard was cleared with the exception of Williamson's grave.

Joseph Williamson's portrait still hangs in Edge Hill Public Library. The most famous image, however, is an old photograph reputedly taken in 1822. This, together with a photograph believed to be of his wife, are both glass-plate images. They were found in what can only be described as a secret hiding place beneath the floorboards of his house. The damaged photograph was reputedly found by Samuel Johnson, the then owner of the house. If the photograph were genuine and some suggest it is not, it would be the earliest portrait photographs ever taken.

The underground caverns

Joseph Williamson retired in 1818, presumably having made enough money by this time. In the years following the end of the Napoleonic wars, there was a depression in Britain and many men were out of work. Williamson felt sorry for them and decided to do something about the situation. Whittington-Egan tells us that he was on the Poor Aid Committee and became annoyed with the sanctimonious attitude of some committee members who went on at length about their own charitable work. He got up and exclaimed, 'How many of you employ labourers?' He then took them out to show them the men he employed who, on this occasion, were engaged in futile tasks above ground but, as time went on, turned to underground excavation.

The Stonehouse Plan and manuscript

The caverns themselves are described in colourful terms by Stonehouse, Hand and Whittington-Egan. Stonehouse describes how the stone was excavated and piers, made of either brick or stone, were constructed to support the roof. He describes a passage 120ft long, 6ft wide and 10 or 11ft high which crossed over other tunnels running north to south. This tunnel lets out onto Mason Street. Stonehouse describes the Smithdown Lane entrances as tiers of arches with a curiously ruined appearance and filled with rubble as they are today. He also describes a deep pit of water, where a woman had drowned a year or two earlier. The pit is surrounded by rubble-filled vaults which are described on the map as a frightful labyrinth. Mention is also made of side alcoves like the bins of a wine cellar and some arches that were walled up.

Stonehouse states that the terrace garden was raised on vaults and the cross-section drawn by the Royal Engineers shows that there were multiple levels to these vaults. On one visit, Stonehouse was shown a large, arched vault in which two carts could pass side by side. Occasionally, there were vertical shafts, covered by grids in the street, to permit light.

Stonehouse gives an account of one of Williamson's houses in Bolton Street, now renamed Shimmin Street. This house stood on arches linked by a tunnel under the road. It was built for a Mr Henderson, an artist, who, according to Stonehouse, was an intimate friend of Joseph Williamson. Williamson also owned property on High Street, now Highgate Street and one of these houses had a coal vault which could take 200 tons of coal. Stonehouse's map does not show an underground link but the Royal Engineer's map shows a second underground link at point A under Mason Street which may have gone to High Street. From this coal vault, an archway led to a lofty vault containing domestic refuse and there was also a pool or tank for the use of the privy above. According to Stonehouse, these houses backed onto Back Mason Street and, on the plan of 1848, they are called St Mary's Place. The 1848 plan also shows a group of buildings labelled 'Joseph's' buildings.

Stonehouse uses colourful terms to describe the labyrinths and passages. He also tells of two complete four-bedroomed houses, one above the other, which are shown in the south-west corner of his map as 'excavated houses, two deep and filled in'. They were linked by a winding, spiral passage, which Stonehouse likens to Petra or Edinburgh.

A tunnel in the north-west corner of Williamson's land, 8ft high and 8ft wide, runs up to Mason Street. Stonehouse's map shows two parallel passages on the northern side of Williamson's property. The most northerly of the passages is labelled 'tunnel to Mason Street' but the second, adjacent to it, is labelled 'passage, vaulted running under two tiers'. Stonehouse states that this tunnel is 60yds long and has several

Joseph Williamson died on the first of May 1840 and was buried in St Thomas's Churchyard in Park Road.

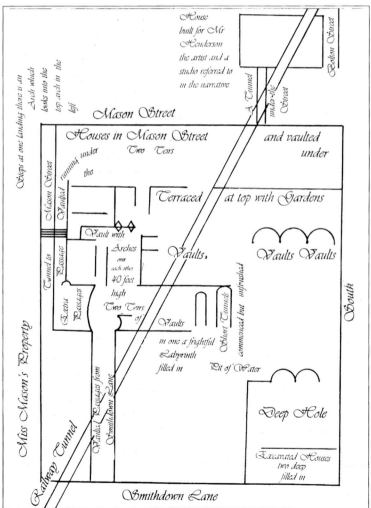

flights of stone steps about two thirds of the way up. His map, which is not drawn to scale, shows only one flight of stone steps halfway along the tunnel and passage. Off this passage to the south, there is large vault at a deeper level and only the top of the arch of the vault links with the passage. Stonehouse tells of a second flight of steps where there is a chute for the disposal of garden rubbish from the gardens above. At the lower, western end, the passage opens out onto the garden and four lofty recesses 4ft deep are described, but these are not clearly shown on the map. Could these be the extra passages labelled on the map? One of these alcoves contained a chimney for the hothouse in the garden above.

Stonehouse's map shows a vaulted passage from Smithdown Lane. We are told that right beside the door, whose location is not clear, was a large brick vault 15ft wide and 9ft high. Although this sounds like the entrance behind the Corporation Stables, it would seem to be too far north, as the arches behind the them lie to the south of the railway line. This vault becomes larger inside, being 25ft high and 40 or 50yds in length. Could this be the feature marked on the map as the vault with arches over each other 40ft high? This appears to be a large wide chamber with a vaulted passage running northwards to the boundary of the property for about 50 or 60ft. The side vault is shown on the map and appears to run under the tunnels and passages on the northern boundary of the property and indeed, Stonehouse states that this is precisely what happens.

The Royal Engineers map shows a large chamber running from west to east with a narrower branch going north to the northern boundary. Stonehouse states that this north-south vault is 36ft wide and 30ft high and partly infilled with debris containing a tunnel that first leads up to Mason Street and then turns to run under the houses bordering Mason Street. Stonehouse's map shows the houses on Mason Street as being 'vaulted under'. This is probably the 'passage, vaulted running under two tiers'. Stonehouse's guide described passages running out to the right and the left and a large square area, 40ft across and open to the sky. Is this the 'open space' Stonehouse described numerous vaults going in all directions. One of these must originally have been 50-60ft high before rubble was dumped on the floor. Stonehouse describes vaults which ran all the way down to Grinfield Street which are now 'broken up and partly destroyed'. The section shows the passages as three tiers, one above the other running from north to south towards Grinfield Street. The railway line cuts the tunnels with a 70-80ft deep

trench. When the Williamson tunnels were first cut and Stonehouse produced his first plan, there was only a small tunnel. This is shown on the 1:1,000 Ordnance Survey map of 1848. During the 1880s this tunnel was widened to take four railway lines, during which process it was changed into a cutting, with only short stretches of tunnel remaining, usually located underneath the roads. This cutting severed the main north-south Williamson tunnel and is shown on the 1:500 map of 1891.

Stonehouse described a large chamber running eastwards with a height of 80ft and a length of 80 to 90ft. Brick arches lined the roof and a massive stone pillar supported three smaller arches, one on top of the other, on either side of the main vault. Another large vault, whose location is not clear on the map, had a raftered roof, which Stonehouse presumed was the floor of a house. Stonehouse's map also shows three arches to the south-east and two to the south-west near a deep hole which presumably correspond to the present arches behind the corporation stables.

The West Lancashire Territorial Forces Association map of 1907

In the early 1900s, the West Lancashire Territorial Forces Association drew their own plans of the tunnels. The soldiers presumably went down into the tunnels with compasses and tape measures to map them. Their interest probably lay in the fact that tunnels ran under the drill hall which was possibly built on the site of Williamson's house. The 1:500 Ordnance Survey map of 1891 shows that the drill hall used to be located on the east side of Mason Street. When the army survey was carried out in 1907, the drill hall had moved over to the west side of the road and was located in the north-east corner of the Williamson property. In 1891 the map also shows a parade ground and modelling shed. The volunteer headquarters occupied another house further along the road. The West Lancashire Territorial Forces Association map shows a tunnel linking the old drill hall to the east and the new drill hall to the west. None of these army premises is shown on the 1:1,000 Ordnance Survey map of 1948.

The West Lancashire Territorial Forces Association map of 1907 shows a relatively simple picture which is almost certainly incomplete due to the amount of rubble blocking the various tunnels. In fact, the rubble and hazards in the tunnels were a cause of great concern in the

Above The above photograph has been commonly assumed to be of Joseph Williamson. A glass-plate image found in a secret hiding place beneath the floorboards of his house together with a photograph supposedly of his wife, the photograph was reputedly taken in 1822. In reality, glass based photography only commenced in 1851 with the introduction of wet collodion plates. The first commercial photographic studio in Liverpool, using the Daguerrotype process, did not commence trading until 1841, well after Williamson's death, leaving little doubt that, although the photograph is used in all references to him, it is not of the 'King of Edge Hill'.

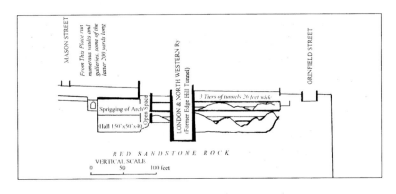

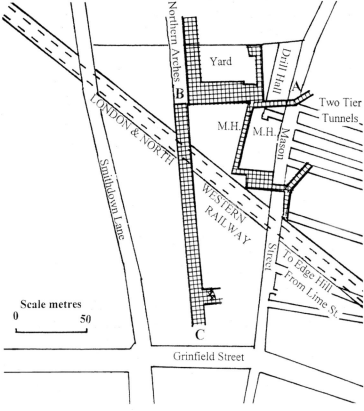

1860s. An article in The Liverpool Porcupine in August 1867 describes the tunnels as 'a great nuisance', claiming that the privies and drains ran straight into the tunnels causing an obvious nuisance. So bad was the situation, that it was reported to the Medical Officer of Health and the Health Committee, whose job it was to seek an abatement order from the justices. It describes the deep pit behind the new Corporation Stables (in 1867) as a cess pool full of offensive water 15ft deep, bringing the threat of disease. The same article is not very complimentary about James Stonehouse (not actually named), who is described as a 'garrulous nonagenarian' who wrote the 'Recollections of Old Liverpool' in 1863.

By November in the same year, the Porcupine was still complaining that nothing had been done. It went on to say that 'week after week, tons of refuse were being added to the accumulating stock in the galleries and caverns beneath the houses in the district'. The implication of the article was that the refuse contained organic waste which 'festered' and threatened 'pestilence'.

The West Lancashire Territorial Forces Association map of 1907 also shows a tunnel going northwards outside the boundary of Williamson's property into what was Miss Mason's land and what is now possibly Albert Street.

The section shows the cross-section along the line A-B-C. This is far from simple with two and three tiers of tunnels being common, many of which are shown partly blocked with rubble. The two-tier tunnels shown in cross-section at the southern end of the site could either be the eastward branch of the main north-south passage near Grinfield Street or the present entrance behind the corporation yard. Since the line of section follows a right angle from A to B and then to C, one can only guess where point B actually is. Could it be where the deep open space is? If that is the case, the tunnel seen in cross-section near Mason Street would probably be the northward-leading tunnel which went under the Mason Street passages to the northern boundary of Williamson's land. The hall with the 'sprigging of arches' above, clearly occupies the wide east-west area which leads east under the drill hall and Mason Street. The dimensions of the hall are given as 150ft by 50ft and 40ft (presumably height). These match some of the dimensions described by Stonehouse.

The Micro-gravity Survey map of 1995

This map was carried out as an undergraduate dissertation by a Liverpool University geology student named Robert Cuss. A gravity survey measures small variations in gravity due to either different rock densities or the presence of cavities beneath the land. An area containing cavities would give a lower gravity reading than the surrounding area. Rob Cuss addressed the Friends of Joseph Williamson on 18 September 1997 and described how this was a particularly difficult survey given the present ground conditions. His results, shown in the map, are ambiguous due to many difficulties such as numerous tunnels being blocked by rubble. Some tunnel features are clearly shown such as the Great Hall in the centre of the map. A tunnel along the northern boundary is clear, along with two possible links to Mason Street, one of which does not match the 1907 map. There are many more tunnels to the south of the railway line but there seems to be little resemblance between the West Lancashire Territorial Forces Association map and the Micro-gravity Survey map in this southern area. The lack of a link between the northern and the southern tunnels could again be due to the amount of rubble inside the tunnels.

Two features stand out as being of interest. The tunnel under Albert Street shown on the West Lancashire Territorial Forces Association map is shown along with a much longer tunnel that goes right under the school and a possible second tunnel. Two other tunnels lie to the east of Mason Street and are shown to be of uncertain existence. They are odd because they seem to run in an unexpected direction, i.e. from north-west to south-east. Rob Cuss also reported subsidence problems shortly after the construction of the Magnet warehouse and in the forecourt adjacent to Mason Street.

The Parkman Survey map of 1995

Parkman, a firm of consultants, carried out a survey on behalf of the Joseph Williamson Society. It incorporates much of the existing evidence as well as the Royal Engineer's survey and the bulk of the micro-gravity results, though one or two new features are incorporated that are not on the micro-gravity survey: the continuation of the tunnels underneath Mason Street and a possible link between the drill hall and Paddington. Could this be the route Williamson took on his way to church at St Mary's Edge Hill? A more recent survey was carried out by Lancaster University but this is not freely available to the public.

Where did Williamson live?

Charles Hand in 1928, tells us that Williamson's house was number 44 Mason Street but that the entries in Gore's and Kelly's directories varied from Number 10 in 1807 to Number 20 in 1839. Hand looked carefully into this issue and tells us that directories record that in:

1807, he lived in number 10 Mason Street
1813, he lived in number 13 Mason Street
1816, he lived in number 24 Mason Street
1821, he lived in number 18 Mason Street
1825 and 1827, he lived in Williamson's Buildings, Smithdown Lane
1829, he lived in number 18 Mason Street
1833, he lived in number 20 Mason Street
1839, he lived in number 20 Mason Street (last entry)

After his death, the auctioneers listed his house as Number 14 Mason Street but Hand comes to the firm conclusion that it was, in fact, number 44 which was still standing in 1926. There is no reason why the houses should not have been renumbered as more houses were built in Mason Street. Thus there is no reason why the house should have been number 44 when Joseph Williamson lived there. Hand thinks this due to the renumbering following the construction of new residences.

Hand goes on to say that the house was subsequently used as a school and then a storehouse and barracks. He also says that he is satisfied that the actual house is number 44 Mason Street and, in 1927, this belonged to Mr Samuel Jones and was used as a machinery store. Number 44 is the building shown as the Volunteer Headquarters on the 1891 map). However, the layout of the building marked 44 does not match Wakefield's drawing which widely accepted as showing Williamson's house. The drawing shows a recessed house with a rounded bay on the northern, right-hand side and a drive in at both ends into a front courtyard, which also contains a small garden with a tree. The only building whose layout matches this picture is the building whose number in the 1891 1:1,000 City Engineer's map was 32 and the building with the embayment on the north side is number 28. There is also a passage shown in the far right-hand side of the yard which is clearly shown on this map.

Entrance to Passage

This vault is on the left of that which runs down in a funnel shape from Smithdown Lane. The hole seen on the right leads to a labyrinth of vaults and strange passages.

The tunnel entrances

Richard Whittington-Egan in 1968 describes some of the entrances to the Williamson tunnels which were in existence 30 years earlier. They are shown in the 1927 1:2,500 Ordnance Survey map and include:

- A tunnel which led from Williamson's back garden to St Mary's Church along which Joseph Williamson and his wife are said to have gone to church. This is one of Williamson's most famous tunnels and, although the possible line of it is shown, we are not exactly sure where it ran.

- Whittington-Egan describes a possible tunnel to a shop at the top of Paddington. If it existed, it may have linked with the tunnel to St Mary's Church. Whittington-Egan describes this as an uncharted entrance and tells the story of a man who started a bottling business in the shop. There were two large cellars, one below the other, in which he could store his bottles. He found that the bottles in the lower cellar were disappearing and, on closer examination, discovered a narrow opening in one corner which led to a tunnel full of empty bottles. In 1926, Charles Hand led a group from the Historic Society of Lancashire and Cheshire into the Williamson tunnels and gained access via a plumber's shop which may have been the same premises.

- Whittington-Egan himself gained access from Mason Street via a garage which had been built on the site of Williamson's old house. This still exists and may provide access in the future when the tunnels are redeveloped.

- The Great Arches above Smithdown Lane lie behind the old Corporation Stables which are about to be redeveloped. The developer is willing to work with the Joseph Williamson Society to preserve and develop part of the tunnel complex.

- Whittington-Egan describes a point of access through a narrow cleft in the railway cutting, which he calls the 'Stephenson Tunnel'. There are stories of the railway engineers meeting the Williamson tunnellers and the two almost certainly crossed and logically there should be two entrances to the Williamson Tunnel, at either side of the cutting but a local man told Whittington-Egan that they are all blocked or waterlogged.

- In 1937, when the flats were being built on the eastern side of Mason Street, Whittington-Egan reports that many of the tunnels were stumbled upon.

- After the war, new houses were constructed in Elm Grove and it is reported that a tunnel 19ft wide and 25ft high was uncovered.

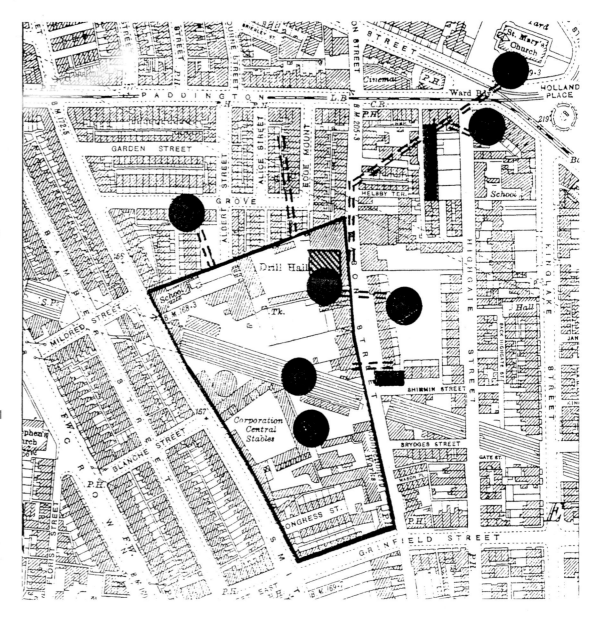

Anecdotes and incidents

Stonehouse tells of the construction of the Railway Tunnel from Edge Hill to Lime Street. The navvies were digging away under Williamson's land when they heard the sound of a pick-axe. Their own tunnel opened up as the Williamson tunnellers crossed their path but we are not told how the intersection of the two tunnels was resolved.

Another anecdote tells of a tenant who complained about damp in her house. Williamson did not necessarily respond promptly to complaints but a few days later, the servant was lighting the fire when the floor opened up and a head popped out, declaring that he was making a sewer to carry away the water.

We are also told of the lady for whom he went out of his way to find suitable accommodation and for whom he provided an instant extension from his own living room. That same lady reported that she frequently heard strange noises from the vaults below, which would not have been surprising if her house was one of those dwellings raftered over a vault.

Many other stories are told about Joseph Williamson and these can be read about in Stonehouse (1863), Whittington-Egan (1939, 1952, 1968) and Hand (1916, 1928).

The tunnels today

Having provided employment during the early part of the nineteenth century, the tunnels became a public nuisance during the second half of the century. Fortunately, little was done to them apart from the fly tipping of rubbish.

The Territorial Army took over much of the site and did little to alter the tunnels. The construction of blocks of flats to the east and houses to the north exposed tunnels which were no doubt filled in and have, therefore, been lost. The construction of a large comprehensive school on the site in the 1960s had little effect, as it lay mainly outside the tunnel area. There was a rumour that the tunnels presented a danger to the school but little has happened and it is still standing.

Whittington-Egan states that the City Council considered opening the tunnels as air-raid shelters but they were rejected as unsuitable and have remained unused ever since.

There is an account of a lorry disappearing into a hole in the yard of the Corporation Stables on Smithdown Lane and of it being left there and the hole filled in. A rectangular area of concrete, indicating where

this must have happened, is still visible today but one of the most famous local stories is of a tunnel linking Williamson's site to the town centre. Naughty boys, stealing from the town centre, are said to have escaped along them. This has recently been given more credence with tales of vaults in the Parr Street/Wolstenholme Square area, near the site of Williamson's tobacco factory. It is said that the concrete floor was built over brick arches which were once a petrol store.

Much of the tunnel network is complete and intact although divided into two sections by the railway cutting.

Today, interest in the work of Joseph Williamson is intense and he is regarded as a major figure in Liverpool's heritage. The Joseph Williamson Society would like to see his importance acknowledged and exploited by the tourist industry and discussions are taking place with Liverpool City Council and other interested groups to look at possibilities. The work needed to clear out the tunnels and make them safe would be expensive and the logical sponsor would be the National Lottery and bids have been prepared. The Joseph Williamson Society and the Friends of Joseph Williamson would also like to see the tunnels listed.

We can only hope that in the future a Joseph Williamson Heritage Centre will stand on the site, with visitors taking a diversion from the city centre, docks and cathedrals to experience a guided tour around this, the most unique of tourist features

Opposite A map of the various access points recorded in the past.

Below An artist's impression of Williamson's house in Mason Street.

Push and pull beneath the ground

The Hydraulic System

Liverpool prospered on the trade created by the port and related industries. These industries had to be powered somehow but during the nineteenth century, electricity was in its infancy and unreliable. Gas had long been used for lighting but not for power and the internal combustion engine had yet to be invented. How else could the cranes, pumps and presses work? The answer was hydraulic power. The dockland city centre area was threaded by a series of pipes, the pressure of which, worked all these machines.

The Liverpool Hydraulic Power Company was based in Athol Street near the Liverpool-Leeds Canal and two pumping stations were located at either end of the system. Furnaces and eight pumping engines created a water pressure of 700 pounds per square inch and the water circulated around the whole system supplying the individual docks, offices and factories. The pumps were capable of delivering 18,000 gallons of pressured water per hour. The network extended north to Canal Street in Bootle and south to Grafton Street in Toxteth where the second pump house was located. The water for the system was probably obtained from the Leeds-Liverpool Canal. There were 30 miles of 2ins diameter pipes and the company pumped an average of three and a half million gallons of water per minute. Inland, branches of the hydraulic system extended east to Scotland Road, St Anne Street and St James Road by St James' Cemetery and one branch extended west to Mann Island.

The map on page 87 shows the dock area was notable for the absence of hydraulic pipes. This was because the docks had their own hydraulic systems. Most people in Liverpool are familiar with the Albert Dock and the Pump House. The Pump House was one of the pumping stations which powered the dock company's own hydraulic system and pipes circulated the dock complex where cranes and hoists, still visible in the Albert Dock, were operated in the same way.

The Liverpool Hydraulic Company was founded in 1887 and, as demand for hydraulic power grew steadily during the early part of the twentieth century, this company took over smaller hydraulic companies. The hydraulic supply was continuous day and night throughout this period, despite problems such as labour disputes. The company also supplied hot water to the docks. It continued to operate into the first half of the twentieth century when it was gradually replaced by other means of power, especially electrically-driven motors.

The uses of hydraulic power

In its day it powered a variety of machines. These included:

- **Basement lifts** in warehouses and commercial businesses to raise goods from the basement to the ground floor level. These were driven by a hydraulic ram directly below the goods platform or lift.
- **Motor car lifts** when the use of the motor car spread during the twentieth century, car mechanics wanted to lift the car off the floor to work underneath as they do today. Hydraulic power was claimed to be safe, steady and reliable.
- **Cranes and hoists** in warehouses were also driven by hydraulic rams. It was claimed that such hydraulic cranes always worked under positive control with no 'overwinding'. Hydraulic power was economical and reliable.
- **Hydraulic pumps** could operate at different speeds for raising liquids and sewage. Such pumps needed little attention and could be started and stopped automatically.
- **Hydraulic capstans** were used for hauling heavy railway wagons and were almost universally adopted due to their inexpensive efficiency. These machines could be operated using a foot valve.
- **Vacuum cleaners** were in their infancy and yet, in 1924, the Liverpool Hydraulic Company claimed that these vacuum cleaners were noiseless and gave the highest vacuums, with no working parts to 'get out of order'.
- **Ejectors** were used to keep wet basements dry. They could remove muddy, gritty or even boiling water from basements. These ejectors had no moving parts and needed little maintenance and could be operated either automatically or manually.
- **Hydraulic pressure-powered fire hydrants** directly using their own water pressure clearly would have had great force.
- **Intensifiers** were described as useful for testing equipment up to 700lbs per square inch or for use in presses.
- **Hydraulic presses** could be used for baling or stamping. The hydraulic press was 'unrivalled' and was recommended for baling cloth and scrap metal.
- **Passenger lifts** of 'modern' construction could be driven by hydraulic pressure and could travel at 600ft per minute! They were said to be simple, safe, economical and smooth-running with low maintenance costs.

The uses of hydraulic power seemed infinite and the system continued to operate until the 1960s. Apparently, the ducts and pipes have been taken over by Mercury Telephones as a means of housing their underground cables.

Opposite Athol Street Pumping Station for the Liverpool hydraulic system.

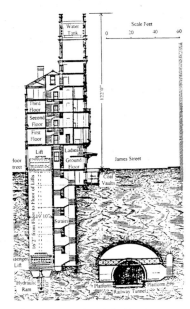

Above A section through the lift at James Street.

Right James Street Water Tower after air raid damage.

Far right The hydraulic lift to James Street Station.

A Lift of the Mersey Railway.

The Wrench Series, No. 7574

The station lifts

The lifts at James Street and Hamilton Square Stations mentioned earlier, were also driven by hydraulic power. A large water tank, 120ft above street level, is located at the top of the tower above the station. Water was fed down to a steam plant to work the pumps to charge the tanks. The hydraulic pressure generated, drove rams beneath the lifts. The hydraulic cylinders for the rams were located beneath the station in solid sandstone. The wells for these cylinders had to be excavated to a depth of 90ft and had a diameter of 40ins. These water towers are no longer needed as the lifts are driven by electricity. The water tower at Hamilton Square is still in place but the one at James Street was damaged during the war and had to be demolished.

Hydraulic power in the dock area

The docks had their own hydraulic power systems. The first use made of hydraulic power was in the Albert Dock, in 1848, and a comprehensive power system was introduced to the Wapping and Stanley Docks in 1850. In the 1860s, hydraulic power was used to operate dock gates. All of the early hydraulic systems were supplied by WG Armstrong of Newcastle. Several other companies, some based in Liverpool, supplied hydraulic machinery later in the century.

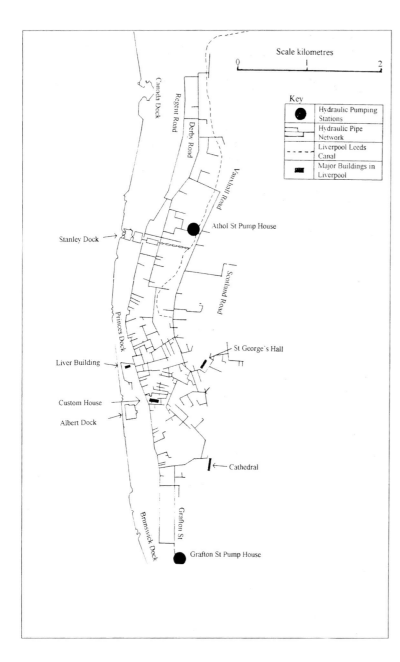

Key

●	Hydraulic Pumping Stations
	Hydraulic Pipe Network
- - -	Liverpool Leeds Canal
▬	Major Buildings in Liverpool

Canada Dock

Regent Road

Derby Road

Vauxhall Road

Athol St Pump House

Stanley Dock

Scotland Road

Princes Dock

St George's Hall

Liver Building

Custom House

Albert Dock

Cathedral

Brunswick Dock

Grafton St

Grafton St Pump House

On the docks, hydraulic power was used for:

- Lifting cargoes
- Opening and closing dock gates
- Operating cranes
- Capstans to haul ships and rail trucks
- Coal tippers
- Swing bridges

Water for the system was supplied from corporation water mains. The pressure was supplied by a head of water driving a ram which was a form of piston. Pulleys operated the machinery such as cranes, some of which were constructed on the warehouse roofs and some of which were mobile. The variations in the pressure of the corporation water mains meant that either the dock company needed to build its own water tower or create the pressure in boiler houses. The latter option was chosen and these boiler houses were located at:

- Wapping Dock – 1856
- Herculaneum Dock – 1864
- Albert Dock – 1878
- Toxteth Dock – 1890

Water pipelines ran throughout the South Docks to power the machinery and, in 1906, the Albert Dock and Wapping Hydraulic Centres were closed, the system relying on the Herculaneum and Toxteth Dock Pumping Stations. As the nineteenth century progressed, hand-driven cranes were replaced by hydraulic cranes although there was competition from steam-driven cranes. By 1930, the electrically-driven cranes were taking over and the days of the hydraulic system were over. The decline in the use of hydraulic power coincided with the decline of the South Docks, as a result of which electrically-driven cranes did not become fully established there.

The Pneumatic Tube System

Until telephones were invented, the fastest way of getting a message to someone was to send a telegraph. In a rapidly-growing city like Liverpool, the greatest delay was in getting the message to the telegraph office and Liverpool had a novel, though not unique, method of doing this. Many older Liverpool residents will be familiar with

Left A simplified version of the network, which extended north to Canal Street in Bootle and south to Grafton Street in Toxteth where the second pump house was located.

Right The Pump House at the Albert Dock drove the dock hydraulic system.

certain shops and department stores, which operated a pneumatic payment system. When you made a purchase, you would hand your money to the assistant who would then put it in a cartridge and place the cartridge in a brass tube, where it was dispatched to a cashier who would send back your change. Such a system operated in Liverpool city centre for the telegraph system.

This system was called the 'Pneumatic Tube System' and was first opened in July 1899. The main telegraph office was located in Victoria Street, where a new Head Post Office has been built. From here, messages would be sent and received, a network of tubes radiating out to the main offices and post offices. The main offices included the Corn Exchange, the Stock Exchange, the Cotton Exchange, Lime Street Station, Central Station and Exchange Station. In all, there were six miles of tubes.

The pipes along which the messages were sent, consisted of a series 9ft, lead-lined, cast-iron tubes, joined very tightly together. The internal diameter of the lead lining was 2¼ins.

The cartridges or carriers for the messages were made of gutta percha with a felt collar at either end to ensure a good seal. The carrier was then propelled around the tubes by air pressure or vacuum, created by two pneumatic engines powered by four boilers which also drove four dynamos. The dynamos generated electricity to provide lighting, power the lifts, drive conveyor belts and charge up the batteries for the telegraphy instruments. The steam also provided heat for cooking and for heating the building. Later on, the steam boilers were replaced by electric motors.

There were several tubes running along each street. All tubes remained separate with some, such as the Corn Exchange link, occurring in pairs; one for sending and one for receiving carriers. Other links, such as the tubes running to the Stock Exchange, would allow two-way travel. The links to many of the offices would only allow one-way travel to the main post-office. In 1914, an average of 10,180 telegraph messages were sent each day. The tubes were maintained by the Post Office engineers but the tubes to the three newspapers were maintained by the newspapers themselves. A separate line, not shown, went south to the Custom House, which was bombed during the war.

It was not uncommon for offices to move premises. When this happened, the tubes had to be diverted. The Pneumatic Tube System operated five days per week and since the tubes lay under the roads and pavements, utilities which needed to dig up roads tended to work at weekends. It was not uncommon for workmen to find a pipe under the road which, at first glance, seemed empty and of no use. The workmen sometimes damaged the pipe during their work and thought no more of it. On Monday morning, the post office engineers would switch on the pneumatic system and it would not work, as it relied on a good seal.

In 1941, the telegraph instrument room was damaged by a bomb and 100 Old Hall Street was requisitioned as a replacement instrument room. The tubes were later recovered from the bombed instrument room and re-erected in the basement of the Main Post Office. In 1952, the bombed Central Bank building in South John Street was restored, renamed Telegraph House and a new instrument room was set up.

By the 1960s, some of the links shown on the map were no longer operating. During the 1960s, the main stations either closed or ceased to use their telegraph links. The declining number of tubes in operation and the general decline in the use of telegrams, meant that the system was no longer an economic proposition and, in 1968, the network was closed, bringing the pneumatic era to an end. Today we take instant, world-wide communication for granted but it was a very different picture 100 years ago!

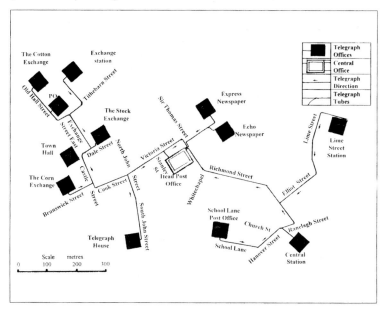

Left A hoist, familiar to Albert Dock visitors, was powered by hydraulic pressure.

Far left The pneumatic telegraph network which took messages from newspapers and offices to the telegraph offices.

It's safer underground

World War II Allied Headquarters

Liverpool made a key contribution to the war effort during the Second World War. Not only did the merchant shipping based in Liverpool keep the nation supplied with food and raw materials, but the Combined Operations Headquarters, controlling the Western Approaches, was based in Liverpool. It was located in the basement of Derby House, part of Exchange Buildings. The construction of Exchange Buildings was started in the 1930s but only Derby House was finished by 1939. The Combined Operations Headquarters was moved north from Plymouth to Liverpool in 1941 at the insistence of Winston Churchill, who had given instructions for the conversion while he was First Sea Lord. After the war, the Combined Operations Headquarters complex was cleared out but the rooms remained more or less undisturbed. Attempts to demolish it failed, as it had been designed to be 'bomb-proof' and 'gas-proof'. The roof of the underground bunker was 7ft thick and the walls 3ft thick and, after one week of demolition work, little headway had been made.

The complex was popularly known as the 'Citadel' or 'Fortress' and was situated on two floors of Derby House. The complex contained over 100 rooms covering an area of 50,000 square feet. It was the inspiration of Sir Max Horton, an ex-World War One submariner, who replaced Sir Percy Noble as commander-in-chief of the Western Approaches in 1942. This control centre was the world's first Combined Operations Headquarters with The Royal Navy, Air Force and Royal Marines co-operating in joint operations. Their job was to monitor the convoys and 'wolf packs' of submarines which, in the early days of the war, were in danger of bringing Britain to her knees.

Arguably the most important room in the complex, was the decoding room, in which the Enigma decoding machine was located. This German decoding machine was recovered, along with the code books, from a sinking 'U' boat. Tragically, the sailors who recovered them, drowned during the operation. Being able to break the code and intercept German military messages, the Combined Operations Headquarters then sent messages to the convoys to help the merchant ships avoid the wolf packs. They were also able to direct the naval vessels whose job it was to hunt them down and destroy them.

Sir Max literally lived on the job, as did several other people. He had a bedroom beside the main operations room and was known to appear at night in rather worn pyjamas. The main operations room – the largest room in the complex – contained various giant maps of the North Atlantic. Convoys and wolf packs could be moved around the maps as they crossed the ocean. Over one thousand personnel worked in the Combined Operations Headquarters, the majority being WRNS and WAAF personnel, who worked day and night in shifts.

In the main operations room today, there is a large table in the form of a map but the maps were actually located on the walls. There were three main maps: one of the North Atlantic, one of the Western Approaches and one of the British Isles. Other maps displayed up-to-date weather information, essential to the aircraft and ships hunting submarines. On the main maps, convoys were plotted and Wrens moved them around using large mobile ladders. The only casualty was WAAF Patricia Lane who fell off a ladder and struck her head and died. Senior Navy and Airforce personnel were based in elevated glass-screened rooms beside the main operations room and their bedrooms were nearby.

Perhaps the most famous event in the history of the building was the hunting down of the Bismark. This was a combined operation between the Royal Navy and Royal Airforce. Arguably the most important engagement was in May 1943, when Convoy ONS 5 met a wolf pack. Twelve merchantmen were sunk, along with seven U boats, the crews of which included Admiral Doenitz' son.

King George VI and Queen Elizabeth visited the Combined Operations Headquarters on 10 November 1942. Sir Max Horton died in 1951 and is buried in Liverpool's Anglican Cathedral.

The centre has been refurbished with authentic materials, having been cleared out after the end of the war. The government provided financial assistance through a 'City Challenge' grant and it is now open to the public and is well worth a visit.

Air raids drive people underground

Everyone in Liverpool knows about air raid shelters. What younger people will not realise is that the drive to provide air raid shelters started well before the war. There are records of debates taking place in 1935 as to what sort of air raid precautions should be taken. There were even proposals to use the new Mersey Road Tunnel as an air raid shelter, should the need arise. Consideration must also have been given to the use of the railway tunnel as a shelter but this was turned down.

Opposite The main operations room contained various giant maps of the North Atlantic. Convoys and wolf packs could be moved around the maps as they crossed the ocean.

Ground Level

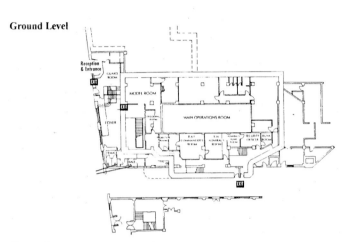

Lower Ground Level

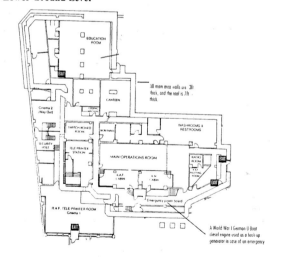

Reports were prepared for the City Council and, in 1938, letters were written complaining that public money could not be spent on air raid shelters. There were proposals to roof over St James Gardens to make a large shelter, followed by a more realistic proposal in January 1939, to roof over narrow, little-used side streets. The City Building Surveyor prepared a report on these shelters – a steel frame would be roofed over with timber. In February 1939, it was estimated that 130,000 shelters would be needed and they would be supplied free to those families with an income of less than £250 per year. Deeper shelters were advocated in May 1939 and by September, 55 trench shelters had been dug and there were plans for 1000 surface shelters. Richard Whittington-Egan stated that at the outset of the war there were enough public shelters for 33,750 people and 180,650 people could be accommodated in domestic shelters. These numbers rose rapidly as the war progressed.

Thousands of Anderson shelters were delivered and a survey was made of cellars which could be converted into air raid shelters. As the war got underway, more trench shelters were dug, railway arches were used and cellars converted. Pressure was mounting for large public shelters, particularly in the city centre. St George's Plateau was one of the first public shelters to be designated with a capacity of 800 to 1000 people. On one occasion, St George's Hall was hit by a bomb and the people fled to James Street Station where they had to force entry as they were not welcome. It was accepted that the station would make a good air raid shelter and the platforms were modified to accommodate the public in the same way as the London Underground Stations. The low-level platform at Central Station was also pressed into service.

The dock area had its own air raid shelter provision as the docks were a prime target for German bombers. Of the 600 brick shelters provided, 71 were destroyed and 40 badly damaged. Remarkably, only ten people were killed. In Gladstone Dock 300 people could be sheltered in pipe culverts. Whittington-Egan tells us that some shelters were used for things other than safety, reporting that one was found full of stolen property.

Stories of camaraderie during the war are common. However, in November 1940, tickets were issued to people who were entitled to use a particular air raid shelter as 'undesirable' elements were causing problems. By January 1941, air raid shelter marshals, either paid or voluntary, were appointed to keep order as reports described 'drunks and rowdies' making life difficult in the shelters and vandalism was costing £100 per week. There were also problems with people who had their own shelter going to the public shelters because they felt they were safer. Such people were turned away. Others preferred the company in the larger shelter or found life there better than home and were reluctant to leave. Health problems arose because of the large numbers of people living close together. If your house was bombed, your Anderson shelter was moved for use elsewhere.

The proposal to build a tunnel under Everton was about to be dropped but the Ministry of Transport gave the project a reprieve as it would have provided an effective and very large air raid shelter. Feasibility studies into deeper shelters were carried out in December 1940 and investigations were made into using the Williamson tunnels but the proposals were turned down.

Blitzed basements were often converted into emergency water supplies for times when the bombing disrupted the mains water supplies. Old wells were recommissioned and new deep concrete reservoirs sprang up all over the city.

Liverpool Castle and the James Street Tunnel

In 1927, Charles Larkin reported on an investigation carried out near the Victoria Monument. A sewer was being driven west towards Preesons Row and the opportunity was taken to examine the remains of the moat of Liverpool Castle. The moat excavations revealed a mass of infill clay and rubble (it was probably filled in between 1704 and 1705). The moat was about 15 to 16yds wide and 22ft deep being cut in rock with steep sides and a ledge in the lower part. The castle itself stood on higher ground and the present site, now containing Derby Square, must have been lowered by quite a considerable amount. Despite heavy rain at the time of the excavation, the water quickly drained away into the rubble along with water which flowed out of vaulted chambers on the north side. St George's Church experienced structural problems because it was built partly on this infill. The first St George's Church was designed by Thomas Steers of dock fame. After 25 years, the tower started to lean, giving cause for concern. Repairs were made but, by 1789, the steeple was leaning 3ft 2ins from the perpendicular. Fears subsided but when the tower parted from the body of the church, it was time to pull it down and build a new one. The foundation of the new tower was laid in 1819 but, by 1825, it was

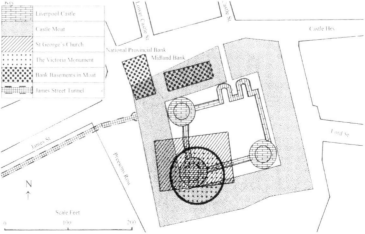

also decided to build a new nave. In 1899, this was also pulled down and the Victoria Monument built on the site. Although the builders of the second church probably underpinned the new tower with substantial foundations, there are signs that the leaning may have set in on the second church. Vaults were located under the church but these were filled in when the church was demolished.

During the last century, there were two banks on the north side of Derby Square. Both of these banks have two sets of basements: a basement and a sub-basement. It is reported that the builders constructed the deep basements since, while excavating in the moats, they needed to get down to solid rock to ensure firm foundations. These basements are now supported on massive lines of columns.

A tunnel leads down the centre of James Street from the Castle to the Mersey shore. When the tunnel was first cut, James Street was narrow and lay entirely to the north of the tunnel. When the street was widened, the tunnel came to be located down the centre of the road. James Newlands described the tunnel when his workmen cleared out mud and found it to be 7ft high, 9ft wide and cut into rock. At Derby Square it was 5ft high and 6½ft wide, running 80yds down to Back Goree. A well-made roadway, 22ft below the surface of the street, ran along the bottom of the tunnel and a drainage channel was cut into the southern side. At Back Goree the tunnel turns northwards, possibly into the old tower or some other defensive work. Several manhole covers can still be seen in the roadway today and one of them appears to be blocked up. The tunnel was surveyed in 1910 by Harold Williams. The channel on the south side was deepened to 6ft to take the sewer and the lower end was blocked up. A proper sewer was laid by James Newlands and his workmen in the bottom of the moat.

Exchange Flags and Vent

There is a large two-storey car park underneath Exchange Flags which has access from Exchange Street East down a series of ramps and a ventilation shaft on the southern side of the Flags. Above the shaft, in Exchange Flags, is the Nelson Memorial, unveiled in 1813. It has a grill structure around the base to provide ventilation. It was relocated, it seems, to provide an outlet for vehicle fumes. Exchange Buildings were originally Georgian but were replaced by a Victorian Structure. The present buildings were started between the wars and, as they were unfinished when the Second World War broke out, were only completed when it was over. The present two-storey car park was once

Right The tunnel under the High Street from the Town Hall to the former police station

Right bottom Town Hall and Exchange Flags.

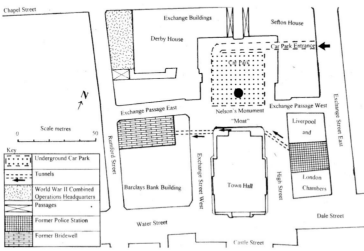

a series of store rooms for oil products for the Valvoline Oil Company based in Exchange Buildings on the corner of Rumford and Chapel Street. Walter Bunn, now retired, started working for Valvoline in 1917. He recalls that 2-3,000 barrels of lubricating oils and grease were stored under the Flags and 'rats as big as cats' had hammers thrown at them by the employees. He also describes the presence of shops down in the basement and a smell of sewage. Further into the basement next to the warehouse of a wine merchant, Bush and Maples, near Rumford Street, there was a tobacconist/sweet shop and two shops displaying cotton samples. The barrels occupied a sub-basement and were raised using the hydraulic lift described earlier. The warehouse of the Valvoline Oil Company moved to Fulton Street opposite Nelson Dock in about 1937 when the Rumford Street building was pulled down. The two-storey car park was the first such underground car park to be built in the city and was reconstructed in 1956 to accommodate the growing number of cars. A temporary office block constructed in 1936 in the middle of Exchange Flags also had to be demolished.

Town Hall Tunnels

The Town Hall of Liverpool was built to a design by John Wood in 1754. Around the sides and rear of the building is a deep area called the 'moat' which allows light to penetrate the basement area where the usual range of utilities are located. Much of this deep moat is very narrow with steps where the floor level changes. At the front, the moat is not as narrow as it would appear, as the pavement is suspended over it and the pedestrians approaching the front entrance to the Town Hall are walking on 'thin air'. At the rear, there are spiral staircases leading down into the moat at each corner. These staircases were not present in the last century as they are not shown on the very detailed 1:500 map published in the last decade of the nineteenth century. In the north-east corner of the moat, there is a tunnel running south-eastwards under the High Street. This tunnel is about three metres high and two metres wide and the walls and arched roof are lined with carefully-trimmed sandstone blocks. The tunnel is blocked off by a brick wall about ten yards in from the entrance.

A similar tunnel is located in the north-west corner of the moat but is blocked off right at the entrance by large, stout, blue doors. This tunnel must have run under Exchange Street West. What were these tunnels for? Some people have suggested that they were routes to take convicts down to the Mersey for transportation to the colonies. If you look carefully at the 1848 map of the Town Hall, the area across the High Street, presently occupied by London Chambers, incorporated a police station and the area now occupied by the magnificent Barclays Bank Building incorporated a bridewell. Could there have been a secure route from the police station to the bridewell using the two tunnels and the moat? Did the Town Hall or the bridewell ever house a court? Records are sparse but its use as a through route from the police station to the bridewell appears to be a likely explanation.

Fazakerley Street 'bridewell'

William Potter's bookshop is located in Fazakerley Street which is off Old Hall Street. It is unusual in that it has what appears to be a bridewell in the basement but, unfortunately, there are no lights, so these basement cells are not generally accessible. There are few records, if any, about its use as a prison or lock-up.

Exchange Station Subway

This subway, built along the line of the old Prussia Street was, at one time, claimed to be the longest in the world. When Exchange Railway Station was built, permission would have been needed to close Prussia Street. The local council and courts have always been reluctant to close off rights of way and, presumably, the subway was an attempt to retain right of access, whilst allowing the closure of the road itself and the construction of the new station. A second and internal subway, for passengers to cross between platforms, lay alongside the Prussia Street subway to the east. This has now closed, along with the station, but the Prussia Street subway has been retained.

There are many other station platform subways, such as that at Broadgreen Station.

The Liverpool Cable Tunnel

The first cables to run under Liverpool carried telegraph wires and one of the first problems was how to insulate the wires. Gutta percha was one of the first successful insulating materials and the cables were laid in cast-iron pipes. When the telephone system started in Liverpool in 1879, overhead cables were preferred. Local wires still run overhead but rapid growth meant that those in the city centre had to go underground. Various insulators were tried and lead was widely used.

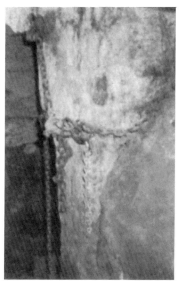

Fazakerley Street 'bridewell' under William Potter's Bookshop.

In the 1960s, polythene replaced lead although it, too, eventually fails. Dark green cast-iron cabinets sprang up all over the city to link the customer to the exchange and petroleum jelly assisted in keeping water out. The Rhodesia crisis in the 1960s led to a sharp rise in the price of copper and aluminium took over as a conductor. Optical fibres are now being used by the cable companies and can carry television and telephone signals. The cables run in ducts which at first were cast-iron, then earthenware, concrete and now plastic. In just over 100 years, the whole system has undergone a series of revolutions leading to today's choice of several reliable and efficient underground links.

Since everyone now uses plastic ducting, different colours are used. They are:

Utility colour used

Telephone	Grey
Water	Blue
Gas	Yellow
Cable TV	Light Green

As a result of the cabling revolution, the ground beneath Liverpool city centre has become a maze of underground networks. Every time a road is changed, this causes problems for the utilities. The Post Office came up with a solution in which a major tunnel would carry the cables in such a way that they would remain undisturbed but would provide access for maintenance and repairs. The tunnel was to run from Lancaster House to Vauxhall Road and then make a dog-leg up to St Anne Street. Cables going north to Bootle, Formby, Ormskirk and Aintree would leave the tunnel at Vauxhall Road and all other cables would leave at St Anne Street. Lancaster House would receive the cables which crossed the Mersey using the Mersey Tunnel.

The project was first recommended in a report in 1965. Work started in 1971 and the tunnel, 1200yds long and 7ft in diameter, was completed in 1975. It had to be deep enough to go under the Waterloo Railway Tunnel and slopes down very gently to the middle. At the centre, in Vauxhall Road, there is a 15ft diameter shaft and the shafts at either end in Back Leeds Street for Lancaster House and St Anne Street are 10ft in diameter. The whole tunnel is lined with pre-cast concrete sections and brackets on the side carry the cables.

The line of the tunnel runs under roads, where possible, in order to avoid private property. A similar problem arose with the access shafts.

The Back Leeds Street site was purchased from the owners of an old warehouse and the Vauxhall Road site was purchased from the Inland Waterways Board as it was on Leeds/Liverpool Canal land. The St Anne Street site was purchased from Liverpool Corporation. Nine boreholes were sunk to check the ground conditions first and work commenced at the Vauxhall Road and St Anne Street shafts. As the tunnelling proceeded, the concrete sections were assembled and the area between the rings and the soil was then grouted (through grouting holes in the rings). The ground was blasted with gelignite and the soil removed was used in the construction of Crosby Marina. Large chambers lie at the base of the access shafts and the various ducts carrying cables lead off from these. Buildings have been constructed above each shaft to house the lifting gantries, power tools and ventilation motors. Air is drawn in at Back Leeds Street and out at St Anne Street, some air being lost at Vauxhall Road.

The tunnel, which cost £800,000, can take 120 three inch cables and is dry and well lit, making it easy to work in.

The Post Office Tunnel under Lime Street Station

The Royal Mail relies on efficient communications and traffic jams need to be avoided by going over or under the traffic. One such example links Copperas Hill directly to Lime Street Station. Before 1974, St Nicholas Parish Church and its junior school, lay on the south side of Copperas Hill. Declining city centre populations led to the closure of the school and church and they were both demolished in 1974, allowing construction to start soon after on a new sorting office. St Nicholas Church had a cemetery and, as elsewhere in Liverpool, permission was needed to disinter the old graves and move them to consecrated ground. This was not a simple matter, as the men clearing the graveyard found a second cemetery, containing lead-lined coffins, below the surface one and permission had only been given to clear the latter.

The slope of the land was such that many of the third, fourth and fifth floor levels of the sorting office, were all at ground level. The sorting office was completed in 1978 and part of the construction included a tunnel to carry the mail to and from the trains at Lime Street Station. Mail from the trains was sent down a spiral chute, which resembled a helter skelter, to a conveyor belt over 12 metres below. The conveyor went along a tunnel under Skelhorne Street and Copperas Hill for a

distance of about 50 metres. Underneath the sorting office, a chain lift hauled the bags of mail to the third floor over twenty metres above, where the mail was sorted and distributed. The outward mail worked in the same way, using a spiral chute, conveyor belt and chain lift.

At that time, the tunnel and conveyor systems were state-of-the-art technology but today, the tunnel is little used and may soon be replaced by an even more sophisticated system. Superstitious people believe the rumours that the tunnel is haunted and are reluctant to venture down into it.

Subways under road

Liverpool's streets have become increasingly busy and crossing them is now a hazardous activity. This can be avoided by:

- Pelican crossings
- Overpasses
- Subways

Pelican crossings are the cheapest option and are very widely used. Unfortunately they break the flow of traffic and many pedestrians are only too willing to 'run the gauntlet' when the lights are on red.

Overpasses were a favoured option in the past and planners in the 1960s and 1970s had a vision of completely separating road and foot traffic. The overhead walkway network was only partly built and sections of it remain around the James Street area. It was never completed and, judging by the fact that most of it has been dismantled, it can be presumed that it was not a spectacular success. For years, a staircase in Moorfields led to an overpass which was never completed. This has now been dismantled. Even the overpasses around the Roe Street Gyratory, which were heavily used, have now disappeared.

Subways are an expensive option, although perhaps easy to construct, when a new road is being built. There are comparatively few subways in Liverpool. Notable ones include:

The Lime Street subway. This is perhaps the simplest having only one crossing. A flight of steps leads down northwards from Skelhorne Street, where it is joined by a ramp running south from the main pedestrian entrance to Lime Street Station. It then runs under Lime Street for about 50 metres to the St John's Shopping Complex. An escalator takes shoppers up to the precinct and market and a ramp runs north-west. The underground station access provides a second tunnel from Lime Street

Left Copperas Hill Sorting Office was completed in 1978 and part of the construction included a tunnel to carry the mail to and from the trains at Lime Street Station. Mail from the trains was sent down a spiral chute, which resembled a helter skelter, to a conveyor belt over twelve metres below.

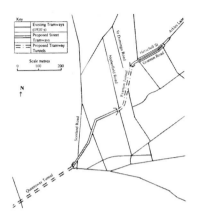

Above and right The Everton Tunnel was meant to provide a link between the East Lancashire Road and the Mersey Tunnel, both of which were opened by the King on the same day in 1934. A very dense housing area separated the two transport arteries and it was thought that a tunnel would avoid costly and unnecessary demolition. However the scheme was abandoned after the War.

Station to St George's Plateau. There are steps at both ends and disabled access is available in the form of a lift giving direct access to Lime Street Station.

The Rocket flyover subway has a more complex layout which reflects the complicated nature of the motorway intersection. There are steps and a ramp leading down to the subway from the shops on Bowring Park Road opposite the 'new' Rocket public house. Two ramps lead down to the subway from the Rocket public house itself and there are both steps and a ramp leading down to the subway from the shops on Queen's Drive. In the centre of the subway, under the Queen's Drive flyover, is a loop for wheelchair access.

The Breeze Hill flyover subway has a large central underpass located under the flyover itself with four points of access. Four roads meet at this point, Queens Drive from the east and west and Rice Lane from the north and south.

Wide Area Traffic Control

This is a system of control boxes linked underground to a central network control to ensure smooth passage of traffic into and out of the city at a given speed. The ducts were laid by the Post Office for Liverpool City Council and the cables were laid by BICC. The piping is plastic and the central control equipment is in Kirkdale Road. It was installed in mid-1970s.

The Williamson Square Tunnel

The Williamson Square tunnel is passed by thousands of people every day but few people notice it. It provides underground access for deliveries and customer collections from Marks and Spencer, Wimpy and the Job Centre. From Whitechapel, the road runs down a slope lined by vertical concrete walls then travels along a tunnel for about 100 metres. At the end is a large cavernous area supported by pillars. This cavern is large enough for a circular roadway to allow delivery and customer traffic to circulate without impeding other traffic. Security staff monitor the traffic and access. A spur leading west, intended for future use, is blocked off. Whether this will ever be used is uncertain at the moment. Originally, there were two approaches but the recent changes to the Roe Street area have reduced this to one.

A similar point of access, also enjoying tight security, is available under the St John's Precinct. Customers and deliveries can gain access from the east end of Williamson Square without traffic complications. This is not the lowest level in the St John's complex as there is a utility level even deeper underground.

The Everton Tunnel – 'The tunnel that never was'

This was described by Maxwell in the Liverpolitan Magazine for 1939 as running from Utting Avenue to Prince Edwin Street; 53ft deep at the Prince Edwin Street entrance and 25ft at the Utting Avenue entrance.

He suggested that it would make a suitable air raid shelter for 54,000 people. Powers were granted under the Liverpool Corporation Act of 1927 and, under these powers, a tramway was to be built along the tunnel. This was meant to provide a link between the East Lancashire Road and the Mersey Tunnel, both of which were opened by the King on the same day in 1934. A very dense housing area separated the two transport arteries and it was thought that a tunnel would avoid costly and unnecessary demolition. The cost at that time would have been two million pounds of which Liverpool Corporation was prepared to pay one quarter. Although trial borings were made, it was never built and the scheme was abandoned after the war, as bomb damage had achieved the demolition needed to construct a dual carriageway link, which the pre-war planners had not been willing to undertake.

The M62 has now replaced the East Lancashire Road as the main entry point into Liverpool but the problem remains of how to link the motorway to the city centre and the Mersey tunnels. Various schemes have been put forward to use the redundant railway tunnels but these have not yet happened.

Electricity Cables under the roads

Everyone needs electricity and we all take it for granted. Cables taking electricity to homes can either go overhead or underground. The latter option is preferred in urban areas but, in the countryside, overhead cables are the norm. Overhead cables are expensive but underground cabling is even more so. For this reason, it is not uncommon to see overhead power cables in urban areas in the United States.

In Merseyside, most cables are located underground. The power is generated by one of the privatised power companies, who distribute the power through a national electricity grid. The voltage of this power is either on 410,000 or 275,000 volts. Power comes into Liverpool along 275,000 volt power cables under the Mersey and from the north-east. Transformers step the power down by stages to 132,000, 33,000, 11,000 or 6,600 volts and then finally to the domestic consumer at 240 or 410 volts. At each stage there is a system of sub-stations which transform the voltage and a separate cable network voltage level. The picture is further complicated by the fact that one substation can perform more than one transformation function i.e. a sub-station might receive 33,000 volt power and transform it down to 11,000 and 410/240 volts.

Cable networks underground are connected to make an integrated

Recommended Cable Burial Depths

The cables which run under the street are different sizes depending on the power load they are carrying. Since 1 October 1988 it is recommended that they are buried at the depths shown in the table below:

Voltage	33,000 volts	11,000 volts	415 volts
In Footpaths	775mm	500mm	400mm
Across Roads	775mm	500mm	500mm
Along Roads	775mm	775mm	775mm

Left Transformers step the power down by stages to 132,000, 33,000, 11,000 or 6,600 volts and then finally to the domestic consumer at 240 or 410 volts.

Left below Laying electricity cables in Everton.

low-voltage network containing network boxes set into the pavement and accessed by manhole covers. The power enters the area at 11,000 volts and needs transforming down to 410/240 volts. This happens at local sub-stations located around the district, inter-linked by cables, from where the 410/240-volt power is delivered to individual homes. Joints or network boxes at the end of road, link the cables to form a network. On newer estates, less network boxes are used. On some older houses, cables run along the houses cleated to the walls but these are gradually disappearing.

Gas mains under the roads

Gas is supplied to the consumer by Transco, a subsidiary of British Gas, which is responsible for storage, pipe-laying, meter-installation, and responding to emergencies such as leaks. They receive the gas from the North Sea Fields and Morecambe Bay. It is then pressurised and sent along large-diameter trunk gas mains at a pressure of 75 bars. Compressors along the route maintain the pressure over long distances. These gas pipes end up at local pressure reduction stations where the pressure is reduced in stages to 0.4–0.7 bars. From these pressure reduction stations, which are frequently located on the site of old gas works such as Garston and Litherland, the gas is sent to the customer who receives it at 25 millibars of pressure. Where possible, pipes are laid under roads at a depth of between 0.6 and 1.5 metres. Large gas mains run under the Mersey Tunnel carrying gas at 25mph. Valves are located throughout the network to enable any part of the system to be closed down for maintenance or safety.

In the past, the pipes were made of cast iron and, as with the water utilities, there is an active programme of pipe replacement. When gas pipes are replaced, strong, flexible, yellow polyethylene pipes, which do not corrode, are used. They can be inserted in the old pipes without even disconnecting the supplies, making pipe-laying much easier and doing away with the need for expensive, inconvenient, large trenches. Since 1977, Transco has replaced 48,000 kilometres of pipes,

resulting in a massive decline in gas leaks. The pipes can be laid by:
- a 'mole' – a self-propelled pneumatic hammer which drags the pipe through the ground,
- thrust boring – which hammers the pipe through the soil where a trench is impossible,
- narrow trenching – where the trench is little larger than the pipe.

The whole network is now computerised and daily or seasonal variations in demand can be catered for by drawing on stocks held in storage. Gas is stored in massive underground salt cavities at Teesside and Hornsea and offshore in the Rough storage field. Locally, it is stored in over 500 gas holders, some of it is as liquid natural gas, at very low temperatures.

Opposite Lister Drive Power Station which has been replaced by a smaller oil fired plant.

Below Clarence Dock Power Station is now demolished. To many Liverpudlians, the chimneys were known as the 'three wickets'.

Catacombs and Crypts

The Metropolitan Cathedral of Christ the King

Liverpool has a particularly large Roman Catholic population, due largely to an influx of Irish immigrants in the 1840s after the Irish Potato Famine. Plans for a Catholic cathedral were put forward as early as the middle of the nineteenth century and, during the 1920s, serious fund-raising efforts were made. At last, the prospect of a cathedral to match Liverpool's status as an archdiocese became more than a dream. Brownlow Hill Workhouse had become redundant as a result of the introduction of old age pensions and more enlightened treatment of the sick and poor. The workhouse site came on the market and was purchased for £100,000. Sir Edwin Lutyens was commissioned to design the cathedral and his design consisted of a large building crowned by a massive dome which would have provided a contrast to the new Anglican Cathedral at the other end of Hope Street. The first stone, laid on Whit Monday 5 June 1933, can be seen today in the well area on the west side of the crypt. The crypt was largely complete at the outbreak of the Second World War but the construction of the cathedral itself ceased. After the war, the cost of completing the Lutyens cathedral was clearly prohibitive and plans were commissioned to reduce the size and cost to realistic proportions. Archbishop Heenan launched a new competition, the terms of which were that the shell was to cost no more than £1,000,000. Sir Frederick Gibberd won the competition and work began in 1962. Within five years the cathedral was complete.

The Crypt beneath the Metropolitan Cathedral of Christ the King

Anyone who has had the opportunity to visit the crypt will be struck by the beautiful but massive arches that seem excessive for such a low structure. A glance at the original plans and model show that although the main body of the cathedral lay to the south, the crypt was designed to carry several extra floors. Today it remains a low structure, half buried in the ground. Hints of a grander design can be glimpsed in the imposing steps leading down to the Blessed Sacrament Chapel and the fine granite exterior which terminates abruptly and incongruously against the sandstone cliffs on the western and eastern sides. Inside, it is a different story. There is a veritable maze of passages and chapels which few people have the opportunity to see in full, not that these rooms are unused.

The Pontifical Chapel houses an altar and the stations of the cross. Unfortunately, a fire in the early 1990s did some damage to the altar area. There is a large display of pictures, plans and photographs showing the construction of the crypt and cathedral. To the south of the Pontifical Chapel is the Chapel of the Relics, which contains the tombs of Archbishops Whiteside, Beck and Downey. The door to this chapel is one of the most fascinating features of the whole cathedral, consisting of a single circular slab of marble which can be cranked open and closed by hand. This stone weighs six tons and represents the stone across the entrance to Christ's tomb.

To the north is the Cathedral Hall, which is used for displays, examinations and a wide variety of functions which include archery and darts matches. At each end of the hall, is a pair of towers containing spiral stairs and capped by pyramids. The staircases are cantilevered and lead up to intermediate or mezzanine floors in which the Green room and the parish rooms are located.

To the west is the Crypt West Chapel, used mainly for concerts, which can house approximately 200 people. Another gem lies here in the form of the stage area which is housed in a half dome-shaped recess made of 'sunray' brickwork (a fan-shaped arrangement of bricks inside the half-dome). The effect is heightened by the way in which the bricks increase in size as the fan radiates out. Smaller chapels are located on either side of the main one and are separated by stout brick pillars and arches.

The Blessed Sacrament Chapel on the east side can house a large number of worshippers or mourners. An organ stands to one side and the altar lies in a second half dome of radiating 'sunray' brickwork. This also has side chapels, one of which is the Lady Chapel.

The central crypt area is occupied by two circular rooms housing kitchens and various utilities. Numerous side passages and staircases lead off this central area and link to all other parts of the crypt.

The windows of the crypt are worth a second glance as the mullions differ, some having only the upper half of the cross whilst others have only the lower half.

Above A window in the crypt with only the upper half of the cross.

Opposite The inclined ramps down into the cemetery in St James Gardens. Catacombs are set into the walls below Gambier Terrace.

◡	Lift
▥	Stairs
⏝	Car Park
• • • • • •	Void (Unused Space)
◀	Six ton rolling stone gate

Right The crypt and basement of the Metropolitan Cathedral of Christ the King.

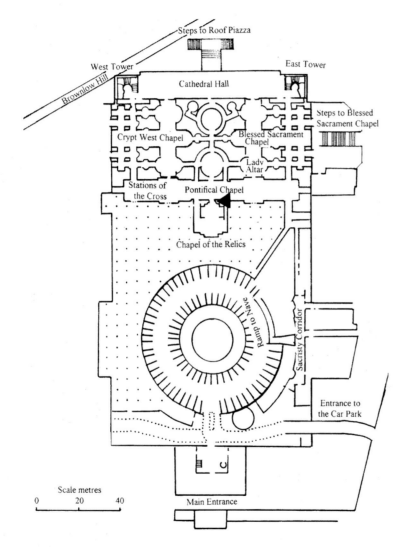

Steps to Roof Piazza

West Tower

Brownlow Hill

East Tower

Cathedral Hall

Steps to Blessed Sacrament Chapel

Crypt West Chapel

Blessed Sacrament Chapel

Lady Altar

Stations of the Cross

Pontifical Chapel

Chapel of the Relics

Ramp to Nave

Sacristy Corridor

Entrance to the Car Park

Scale metres

0   20   40

Main Entrance

Beneath the Metropolitan Cathedral of Christ the King

Flights of stairs from the crypts lead up into the lower part of the main cathedral. The largest area below ground is devoted to car parking – few other cathedrals can boast this facility. A large entrance to the car park is located in the south-east corner and traffic circulates in a clockwise direction. This subterranean area also contains numerous workshops and stores and access can be gained up into the main entrance of the cathedral either by stairs or lift. The sacristy corridor, containing offices and other function rooms, runs from the car park to the crypt, with access to the cathedral via stairs or a ramp. The underground area, as well as housing utilities, contains large voids which are largely inaccessible and generally unused. The basement of the main cathedral is less maze-like but contains numerous doors and poorly-lit passages.

Anglican Cathedral

The Anglican Cathedral, or the Cathedral Church of Christ, is built on solid rock and has no crypt but there are lower floors. The Lady Chapel is sunk at a deeper level than the nave and is located at the south-west end of the cathedral. It is richly decorated with stained glass and carved figures and is used for smaller services and concerts. Also at the southern end, are the choir room, offices and numerous utility rooms.

The central area underneath the nave is almost as maze-like as the Metropolitan Cathedral. The western rooms are used for services, particularly by the Presbyterian congregation of St Andrews, whose church in Rodney Street burned down. On the eastern side, there is an educational area with a lecture theatre and stage and store rooms and workshops underneath. There are two lifts to take people up to the main nave and one is powered by hydraulic rams whereas the tower lifts use cables. A third lift which has been proposed near the education area to take people up to the high balcony level would also use hydraulic rams to avoid unsightly cables. Since this lift will rise to a much greater height, the rams will telescope and will only need a thirty-foot-deep pit to house the ram.

St James Gardens Tunnels

Most Liverpudlians know that the site of the Anglican Cathedral is on high ground above the former quarry from which much of the stone for the construction of Liverpool was hewn. A volume of Kaleidoscope, published in 1928-29, describes how the stone for the old dock was obtained from this quarry and Bailey, in 1916, states that the stone for the Liverpool Town Hall and several Liverpool churches also came from here. When the quarry was closed, it was converted into a cemetery, although one cannot imagine that the floor of the quarry offered easy ground for the sextons to excavate. Many famous people lie buried here and many of the gravestones still exist, lining the sides of the present St James Garden, behind the cathedral. Cornish's Strangers' Guide, published in 1838, describes how the quarry was given to the Diocese of Liverpool on 12 January 1829 and £20,000 was raised by public subscription for the improvement and landscaping needed to make a cemetery.

How did the early quarrymen get their stone out? The steep inclines from Gambier Terrace, shown on the 1848 map, were not present in 1803. Today, most visitors to the park use the steep walkway to the north of the cathedral that goes through a tunnel hewn out of solid rock. Ordnance Survey maps label it as a 'natural arch' which it is not, as the quarrymen's chisel marks can clearly be seen in the roof and walls of the tunnel. This steep path follows the slope of the rock layers or bedding planes. The tunnel is about 20 metres long and 3 to 4 metres high with vertical rock walls lining the pathway above and below it. Being steep and narrow, this route is unlikely to have been used by stone carts or hearses. It is more likely to have been used by cemetery visitors on foot.

If you continue down to the bottom of the path, turn left and look back underneath the path and the 'natural arch' and you will see that there is a second tunnel immediately underneath the 'natural arch' on the path, which seems to go straight underneath the northern end of cathedral. It is wider (about 4 metres) than the 'natural arch' and has a low, stone-lined arch about 3 metres high. The walls of this tunnel are cut from the solid sandstone and the entrance is now bricked up. It has been suggested that this was the quarrymen's route but the author has been unable to find any reference to it. The stone may have been loaded onto carts and taken under St James Mount, presumably into what was St James Road and is now the open area near the west door of the cathedral. Horwood's map of 1803 shows a second stone

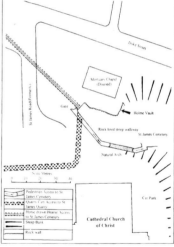

Above The maze of tunnels at the northern end of the Anglican cathedral.

Top A tunnel underneath the northern end of the Anglican Cathedral which was possibly used by quarry men to remove sandstone.

Left The 'natural arch' to St James Gardens.

quarry to the west on what was once Rathbone Street. Could this quarrymen's tunnel have emerged in this old quarry? Exactly where it went we cannot now be sure. This tunnel may have become disused and bricked up when construction of the cathedral commenced. Baynes' illustration in a publication by Fisher in 1839 clearly shows the north end of the quarry but no tunnels, whereas an illustration by Herdman published in 1843 clearly shows a tunnel entrance in a picture dated 1790.

The main route used by the hearses bringing the corpses for burial seems to have been via a third tunnel which lies in the north-west corner of the cemetery and is now largely hidden by ivy. This tunnel, cut from the sandstone, is narrower – about three metres wide and four metres high – and the roof arch is lined with carefully-dressed stone. It used to run under St James Mount to Duke Street but is now blocked off about 20 metres into the tunnel with the entrance itself walled off with massive blocks of yellow sandstone. Again, we cannot be sure exactly where it went but it seems relatively straight. Bailey in 1946 describes two entrances, one at the southern end of the quarry and the second at the northern end which comes from the junction of Duke Street, Rodney Street and St James Road. He states that the tunnel had two 'eyes' to admit light and air and that on each side of both entrances was a pair of carved stone lions. He also states that the tunnel almost runs under the Doric Temple which itself was on the site of a former windmill. In a volume of Kaleidoscope published in 1928-29, the main entrance is described as a tunnel coming from the top of Duke Street, a little to the left of the steps leading up to St James' Walk. This tunnel was 80yds long and lit by only one opening in the roof. Since Herdman shows this tunnel clearly in 1790, it must have been used by the quarry traffic as well as the hearses.

When powered vehicles came into use, they could use the eastern approach from Gambier Terrace where there is a set of zigzagging roads. Horses would have found this route very steep and difficult to negotiate. Powered trucks could cope with the steep slope and narrow turns much better. The terraces formed by this road still exist and were present on the 1848 Ordnance Survey map but not Horwood's map of 1803.

Underneath these terraces and at various points around the cemetery are numerous catacombs. They are graves or vaults cut into the wall of the quarry in which the deceased members of the families of Liverpool worthies were entombed. One of these catacombs contains some members of the family of Samuel Holme, mayor of Liverpool from 1852 to 1853. He and his wife Elizabeth died in Bath but were buried here along with six of their fourteen children. These children all died young; three in infancy, one aged thirteen and the other two in their twenties.

The central arch has a famous spring above which is a stone on which there is an inscription which is difficult to decipher. In 1969 Richard Whittington-Egan stated that it read:

> 'Christian reader view in me
> An emblem of true charity
> Who freely what I have bestow
> Though neither heard, nor seen to flow
> And I have full returns from heaven
> For every cup of water given'

The most famous resident of the cemetery is William Huskisson, MP for Liverpool, who can claim to be the first railway accident fatality.

Liverpudlians underground

Churches come and go as congregations grow and decline. Old maps of Liverpool give great prominence to the number of fine churches located in the city. As the city centre evolved into a commercial and retail centre and the residents moved out, many churches had to close. The land they stood on became valuable and was converted to a more profitable, secular use. Many of these churches had cemeteries in which the deceased were supposed to 'rest in peace'.

In 1885, the Dock Road at St George's Gate was widened and many bodies had to be removed from St Nicholas Churchyard and reburied in Everton Cemetery. A granite plaque, set in the boundary wall facing the river, records this event.

In 1922, St Peter's Church in Church Street was demolished and, again, the churchyard had to be emptied. Forty thousand bodies were removed, my own grandfather being one of the men brought in to remove them. He told of a coffin which, when opened, was found to contain the remains of a beautiful young girl who had died long ago. As the coffin lid was raised and the air rushed in, her face collapsed and disintegrated into dust. Top Shop and various other retail outlets now occupy the site but observant Merseysiders will know of the brass cross set in the pavement and the cross-keys of St Peter high up on the pediment.

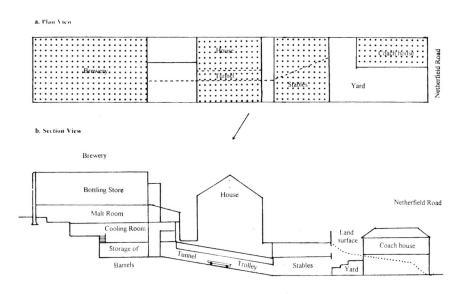

Above *The brewery in Netherfield Road.*

The new sorting office in Copperas Hill was opened in 1977 on the site of St Nicholas Roman Catholic Church which was demolished in 1973. The authorities were somewhat surprised to find a second graveyard located under the one on the surface and two thousand bodies had to be cremated.

Many gardens occupy former cemeteries. What remains of St Nicholas Churchyard provides one of the few quiet green spaces in the city centre for local office workers. Similarly, few people using St John's Gardens behind St George's Hall for recreation or a short cut, stop to think that this was a graveyard from the old St John's Church, built in 1784. The burial ground was closed in 1865 having received 82,500 souls and the church was demolished four years later, making way for the garden to be designated in 1904. Grant's Garden in West Derby is located on the site of the former Necropolis cemetery opened in 1825 and was converted into a garden in 1914.

It has already been stated that St James Cemetery was designated in 1829 from its former use as a quarry. Burials ceased in 1970 and it is now a pleasant, although in places overgrown, garden.

The Everton Brewery

Everton is built on one of the steepest ridges in Liverpool which, over the years, has caused many problems for transport and construction in the area. During the last century, a novel solution was found in a brewery located at Number 216 Netherfield Road by building into the side of the hill. It consisted of a building with four floors. The top two floors contained the main brewing works, the malt room and bottling stores whilst the lower two floors were located underground and housed the cooling room and barrel store.

The main building was connected to the stables and coach house on Netherfield Road by a tunnel that was cut out of solid rock with a roof lined with five courses of brick. The arch was quite low, only 5ft 6ins at the crown, and it was 8ft wide. A tramcar was used in the tunnel and was raised and lowered using a rope hoist worked by an engine.

One of the key features of the tunnel was that when both end doors were open, a strong updraft occurred which cooled the beer in the cooling room. Unfortunately, the brewery was burnt down in 1879 and there were lengthy deliberations over an insurance settlement. It is no

Above The massive brick arches which carry the weight of St George's Hall.

Right Cross section of St George's Hall showing the basement arches.

Opposite top The old quayside of Herculaneum Dock with casemates at the far southern end.

Opposite bottom One of the casemates at Herculaneum Dock is used as a motor vehicle workshop.

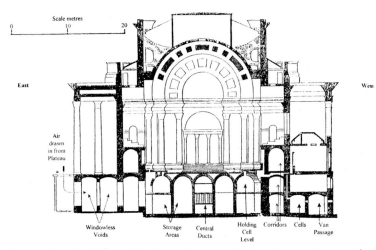

longer there and cannot be located on any of the subsequent maps of the area and it is not known what happened to the tunnel.

Freddie O'Connor in his book 'A Pub On Every Corner', describes a ginger beer manufacturer, Mr Dugdale, with a premises at 218 – 220 Netherfield Road and states that it was in existence in the 1880s. His description matches the above structure together with the buildings and trolley. To have been there in the 1880s, it must have been rebuilt after the fire but it cannot have survived long. He also states that it could be used for the brewing of beer as well as the manufacture of ginger beer.

Underneath St George's Hall

Before St George's Hall was built, a tri-annual three-day choir festival was held in St John's Church Hall, in what is now St John's Gardens. A decision was made to build a fine new hall to house this festival. The architect who won the architectural competition was a young man called Harvey Lonsdale Elmes. Construction work started in 1841 but tragically, Elmes died of consumption in 1847 before it was finished. The law courts were completed in 1851, the Great Hall in 1854 and the concert room in 1855. It seems a massive undertaking for a three-day choir festival but Liverpool has been left with a fine neo-classical building.

Below the Great Hall are two main levels or basements. The lowest level houses the heating and ventilation system. The heating system had two main boilers which burned coke instead of coal because coal

smoke rising above the building would have spoilt its classical look. The boilers heated water and could also produce steam in radiators and pipes which, in turn, heated the air which was circulated by large fans driven by a steam engine. These fans looked like the paddles from a Mississippi paddle steamer. Underneath the ground-level floor is a labyrinth of passages which acted as an early air-conditioning system. The building was lit by gaslight and the vapours needed an escape route. A sophisticated system of extraction was developed by Dr DB Reid from Edinburgh, who had worked on the House of Commons, newly reconstructed after the Great Fire. Fresh air was drawn in through large grills on St George's Plateau and then led underground. (It was considered undesirable to draw air from the direction of St John's Cemetery where so many cholera victims had been buried). It was drawn along passages, the flow being controlled by canvas doors which acted as valves, then channelled to the main rooms. The contaminated air was drawn up to the roof level at four main points. These vertical ducts had several separate flues for coke smoke and exhaust fumes. At one point, a plan was put forward to build a massive chimney where Wellington's Column now stands. This chimney would have drawn the coke smoke downwards, along a tunnel and under William Brown Street but it was never built. Smokeless fuel partly solved the problem.

In 1895, electricity replaced gas as a source of light. This created much less stale air and the large fans became redundant as it was no longer necessary to exhaust 100% of the air. More recently, the coke furnaces have been replaced by large gas boilers but, where possible, the original ducts and pipes have been retained to avoid the destruction of this unique Victorian heating system.

The other main use for the building was the Crown Courts. These courts were transferred to the new Queen Elizabeth II Law Courts in 1984. Defendants who were accused of serious crimes were tried in the St George's Hall Crown Courts, especially in the court in the south zone. Florence Maybrick, of fly-paper poison fame, was tried for murder in 1889, as was William Wallace, the Prudential Assurance agent, in 1931. Defendants were brought in by horse and closed van from Walton Jail. They would enter the van passage on the west and be held in a row of cells on the western side of the lowest floor level. Men and women were housed in separate cells. From here, the defendants would be transferred up special staircases to a holding cell on the mezzanine level. When the court was ready, the defendant would be taken up directly into the main body of the court. If they were found guilty, they might be transferred to the condemned cell at the southern end of the cell block. These cells are still in place, complete with the graffiti scrawled by idle hands. Some of them have been cleaned up for use as film sets.

On the western side on the mezzanine level are kitchens and staff rooms. Some of the central area of both the lower levels is used for storage but much is unused. Perhaps this is where the air raid shelter was located during the war? Massive brick pillars, brick arches and thick brick walls support the higher floor levels, columns and flights of steps.

There are three entrances to the building. The William Brown Street entrance and its foyer serve the Small Court Room, the Lime Street entrance serves the Great Hall and the St John's Lane entrance serves the south end of the building but has rarely been used. All the entrances have steps either externally or internally to the main ground floor in an essentially classical concept designed to give grandeur of access.

When the law courts were closed and transferred, the question arose of what to do with the building. It is now used extensively for concerts and functions and is ideal as a Victorian film set. Most Liverpool residents may well have seen the magnificent Great Hall and its floor and have marvelled at the organ and Small Concert Room. The lower floors lack the beauty and elegance of the Great Hall but are no less fascinating. They hold an eerie magic and are a vital part of Liverpool's history and architecture.

The Herculaneum Petroleum Stores

The most southerly of Liverpool's South Docks was the Herculaneum Dock, built in the late nineteenth century. It consisted of a narrow L-shaped dock off which there were four graving docks. Railway tracks ran along the quays. At the rear and along the southern side are a series of rock-hewn caverns variously described as magazines or casemates. There are sixty of these casemates and they were capable of holding 60,000 barrels of petroleum in total. The walls and roofs are all cut from solid red sandstone. Each casemate is 51ft deep, 19ft high and 20ft wide, and separated from its neighbour by 5ft thick rock walls. The casemates had high sills across the front to prevent petroleum leakage even if the entire contents was spilt.

Many people think that the casemates were developed to house

explosives for the Napoleonic Wars. There was a dock located here during that time but it was to serve local copper smelters and later pottery manufacturers and shipbuilders. Acts of Parliament to develop the site were passed in 1840 and 1846 and the graving docks and half-tide docks were opened in the 1860s. The branch dock, alongside which the casemates were located, was not built until 1882. The construction of this branch involved cutting a 70ft high rock face, and the excavation of the casemates to provide secure storage for petroleum products which had already been imported for some years. Therefore, the casemates could not have been used for Napoleonic War explosives but they were used to store other inflammable materials such as resin, turpentine and explosives. The development of bulk storage tanks for petroleum products in the 1890s gradually made the casemates redundant in terms of their original purpose. They proved particularly useful for the storage of explosives during the two World Wars and later for radioactive substances. They were also used as bonded wine warehouses and cotton stores.

Similar structures can be found inland of the old Brunswick Dock but these are not cut in solid sandstone, they were constructed against the back wall of the dock and are built from stone and brick. They are shallower than those at Herculaneum Dock and, in some cases, several magazines have been joined to neighbouring ones whilst others are separated by brick walls. These now lie behind the Renault motor agency on the new Dock Road. Although many do not appear to be in use, they have great potential and seem to be in a good state of repair. Today, the Herculaneum Dock has gone: it was filled in during the early 1980s. The quays, complete with iron bollards, are still visible and many of the rail tracks survive although they have not been used for many years. The casemates belonged to the now disbanded Merseyside Development Corporation and a few are used for workshops and warehouses.

Conclusion

Right top Beneath the Wapping Warehouse are arches to match St George's Hall and the Metropolitan Cathedral crypt.

Right bottom The Cavern Club, Liverpool's most famous underground location. There are so many steps one must ask if it is below the level of the old pool.

Liverpool is a bit like an iceberg. We know its tip with its familiar streets and buildings but beneath the surface is an unknown world of pipes, cables, tunnels and basements. No map exists of this Liverpool under Liverpool and, hopefully, this book has given some shape to the subterranean city. What became clear during the research for the book is that there is still a considerable amount of mapping left to be done. William Pring recently wrote to the Liverpool Echo about a tunnel he had excavated in Lydia Anne Street some fifty years ago. Working on the basement of a house, he discovered a tunnel with a brick-laid roadway. "We investigated further and found it was a roadway wide enough for a horse and a wagon and, at one point, had a heavy steel door across." The Council was informed but showed little interest and Mr Pring took no further action. So what was the tunnel and is it still there?

No doubt other readers will have their own knowledge of hidden tunnels and cellars and this information can be incorporated in future editions. The national interest surrounding the Edge Hill tunnels has revealed how little we know both about Joseph Williamson and the extent of his tunnels. Popular mythology has smugglers' tunnels running from virtually every public house in the city down to the docks. Excavation of Williamson's tunnels might eventually resolve some questions and, no doubt, new finds will add to our picture of underground Liverpool. Nevertheless, it is unlikely that we will uncover all of the city's hidden secrets as new layers of development obscure and fill-in old layers.

What we do have, even if incomplete, is a fascinating record of how we have used the land beneath us – for water and power supplies, sewage disposal, transport, communications, safety, storage, incarceration, entertainment and, if legends about smuggling are to be believed, criminal activity. *Underground Liverpool* is the first publication to map these many activities and is, I hope, a starting point for further research and exploration into the city beneath our feet.